MW01232416

This logo means that this courseware has been approved by the Microsoft® Office Specialist Program to be among the finest available for learning Microsoft Word 2003. It also means that upon completion of this courseware, you may be prepared to take an exam for Microsoft Office Specialist qualification.

What is a Microsoft Office Specialist? A Microsoft Office Specialist is an individual who has passed exams for certifying his or her skills in one or more of the Microsoft Office desktop applications such as Microsoft Word, Microsoft Excel, Microsoft PowerPoint, Microsoft Outlook, Microsoft Access, or Microsoft Project. The Microsoft Office Specialist Program typically offers certification exams at the "Core" and "Expert" skill levels. The Microsoft Office Specialist Program is the only program in the world approved by Microsoft for testing proficiency in Microsoft Office desktop applications and Microsoft Project. This testing program can be a valuable asset in any job search or career advancement.

To learn more about becoming a Microsoft Office Specialist, visit **www.microsoft.com/officespecialist**. To learn more about other Microsoft Office Specialist approved courseware from Element K, visit **www.elementkcourseware.com**.

*The availability of Microsoft Office Specialist certification exams varies by application, application version, and language. Visit **www.microsoft.com/officespecialist** for exam availability.

Microsoft, the Microsoft Office Logo, PowerPoint, and Outlook are trademarks or registered trademarks of Microsoft Corporation in the United States and/or other countries, and the Microsoft Office Specialist Logo is used under license from owner.

Element K is independent from Microsoft Corporation, and not affiliated with Microsoft in any manner. This publication may be used in assisting students to prepare for a Microsoft Office Specialist Exam. Neither Microsoft, its designated program administrator or courseware reviewer, nor Element K warrants that use of this publication will ensure passing the relevant exam.

NOTES

Microsoft® Word 2003

Level 2

Nancy Curtis

Microsoft® Word 2003: Level 2

Part Number: 084361
Course Edition: 1.0

ACKNOWLEDGMENTS

Project Team

Content Developer: Nancy Curtis • **Content Manager:** Cheryl Russo • **Content Editors:** Peter Bauer and Christy Johnson • **Material Editors:** J-P Altieri and Lance Anderson • **Graphic/Print Designer:** Tracie Cole • **Project Technical Support:** Michael Toscano

NOTICES

HELP US IMPROVE OUR COURSEWARE

Your comments are important to us. Please contact us at Element K Press LLC, 1-800-478-7788, 500 Canal View Boulevard, Rochester, NY 14623, Attention: Product Planning, or through our Web site at **http://support.elementkcourseware.com**.

MICROSOFT® WORD 2003: LEVEL 2

Contents

Microsoft® Word 2003: Level 2

CONTENTS

ABOUT THIS COURSE

In the first course in this series, *Microsoft Word 2003: Level 1,* you gained all the basic skills that you need to create a wide range of standardized business documents. If you use Microsoft® Word 2003 on a regular basis, then once you have mastered the basic skills, the next step is to improve your proficiency. To do so, you can customize and automate the way Microsoft® Word 2003 works for you, and you can improve the quality of your work by enhancing your documents with customized Microsoft® Word 2003 elements. In this course, you will increase the complexity of your Microsoft® Word 2003 documents by adding components such as customized lists, tables, charts, and graphics. You will also create personalized Microsoft® Word 2003 efficiency tools.

Mastering the skills in this course will help you if you are preparing for Microsoft Office Specialist certification in Microsoft® Word 2003. But, more important, this course will help you go beyond the basics of word processing to enhance your Microsoft® Word 2003 documents with sophisticated components such as tables, charts, customized formats, and graphics. It will also help you create your own Microsoft® Word 2003 efficiency tools to produce attractive and effective documents with less time and effort than you've ever needed before.

Course Description

Target Student

This course was designed for persons who can create and modify standard business documents in Microsoft® Word 2003, and who need to learn how to use Microsoft® Word 2003 to create or modify complex business documents as well as customized Word efficiency tools. It will be helpful for persons preparing for the Microsoft Office Specialist exams for Microsoft® Word 2003.

Course Prerequisites

Students should be able to use Microsoft® Word 2003 to create, edit, format, save, and print basic business documents that contain text, basic tables, and simple graphics. Students can obtain this level of skill by taking the following Element K course:

- *Microsoft Word 2003: Level 1*

How to Use This Book

As a Learning Guide

Each lesson covers one broad topic or set of related topics. Lessons are arranged in order of increasing proficiency with *Microsoft® Word 2003*; skills you acquire in one lesson are used and developed in subsequent lessons. For this reason, you should work through the lessons in sequence.

We organized each lesson into results-oriented topics. Topics include all the relevant and supporting information you need to master *Microsoft® Word 2003*, and activities allow you to apply this information to practical hands-on examples.

You get to try out each new skill on a specially prepared sample file. This saves you typing time and allows you to concentrate on the skill at hand. Through the use of sample files, hands-on activities, illustrations that give you feedback at crucial steps, and supporting background information, this book provides you with the foundation and structure to learn *Microsoft® Word 2003* quickly and easily.

As a Review Tool

Any method of instruction is only as effective as the time and effort you are willing to invest in it. In addition, some of the information that you learn in class may not be important to you immediately, but it may become important later on. For this reason, we encourage you to spend some time reviewing the topics and activities after the course. For additional challenge when reviewing activities, try the "What You Do" column before looking at the "How You Do It" column.

As a Reference

The organization and layout of the book make it easy to use as a learning tool and as an after-class reference. You can use this book as a first source for definitions of terms, background information on given topics, and summaries of procedures.

Microsoft Word 2003: Level 2 is one of a series of Element K courseware titles that addresses Microsoft Office Specialist (Office Specialist) skill sets. The Office Specialist program is for individuals who use Microsoft's business desktop software and who seek recognition for their expertise with specific Microsoft products. Certification candidates must pass one or more product proficiency exams in order to earn Office Specialist certification.

Course Objectives

In this course, you will add complexity to Microsoft® Word 2003 documents and create personalized efficiency tools in Microsoft® Word 2003.

You will:

*   manage data in lists.
*   customize tables and charts.
*   customize formatting.
*   work with custom styles.

- modify pictures in a document.
- create customized graphic elements.
- control text flow.
- automate common tasks.
- automate document creation.
- perform mail merges. ,

Course Requirements

Hardware

For this course, you will need one computer for each student and one for the instructor. Each computer will need the following minimum hardware components:

- A 233 MHz Pentium-class processor if you use Windows XP Professional as your operating system. 300 MHz is recommended.
- A 133 MHz Pentium-class processor if you use Windows 2000 Professional as your operating system.
- 128 MB of RAM.
- A 5 GB hard disk or larger if you use Windows XP Professional as your operating system. You should have at least 600 MB of free hard-disk space available for the Office installation.
- A 3 GB hard disk or larger if you use Windows 2000 Professional as your operating system. You should have at least 600 MB of free hard-disk space available for the Office installation.
- A floppy disk drive.
- A mouse or other pointing device.
- An 800-x-600 resolution monitor.
- Network cards and cabling for local network access.
- Internet access (see your local network administrator).
- A printer (optional).
- A projection system to display the instructor's computer screen.

Software

- Either Windows XP Professional with Service Pack 1, or Windows 2000 Professional with Service Pack 3.
- Microsoft® Office Professional Edition 2003.

Class Setup

For Initial Class Setup

1. Install Windows 2000 Professional or Windows XP Professional on an empty partition.

   - Leave the Administrator password blank.

   - For all other installation parameters, use values that are appropriate for your environment (see your local network administrator if you need details).

2. On Windows 2000 Professional, when the Network Identification Wizard runs after installation, select the option Users Must Enter A User Name And Password To Use This Computer. (This step ensures that students will be able to log on as the Administrator user regardless of what other user accounts exist on the computer.)

3. On Windows 2000 Professional, in the Getting Started With Windows 2000 window, uncheck Show This Screen At Startup. Click Exit.

4. On Windows 2000 Professional, set 800 x 600 display resolution: Right-click the desktop and choose Properties. Select the Settings tab. Move the Screen Area slider to 800 By 600 Pixels. Click OK twice, and then click Yes.

5. On Windows 2000 Professional, install Service Pack 3. Use the Service Pack installation defaults.

6. On Windows XP Professional, disable the Welcome screen. (This step ensures that students will be able to log on as the Administrator user regardless of what other user accounts exist on the computer.) Click Start and choose Control Panel→User Accounts. Click Change The Way Users Log On And Off. Uncheck Use The Welcome Screen. Click Apply Options.

7. On Windows XP Professional, install Service Pack 1. Use the Service Pack installation defaults.

8. On either operating system, install a printer driver of your choosing as the default printer (a physical print device is optional).

   - For Windows XP Professional, click Start and choose Printers And Faxes. Under Printer Tasks, click Add A Printer and follow the prompts.

   - For Windows 2000 Professional, click Start and choose Settings→Printers. Run the Add Printer Wizard and follow the prompts.

9. If you do not have a physical printer installed, right-click the printer and choose Pause Printing to prevent any print error messages.

10. Run the Internet Connection Wizard to set up the Internet connection as appropriate for your environment, if you did not do so during installation.

11. Log on to the computer as the Administrator user if you have not already done so.

12. Perform a Complete Install of Microsoft® Office Professional Edition 2003

13. Minimize the Language Bar if it appears.

14. On the course CD-ROM, open the 084_361 folder. Then, open the Data folder. Run the 084361dd.exe self-extracting file located within. This will install a folder named 084361Data on your C drive. This folder contains all the data files that you will use to complete this course.

15. Move all the data files and the Custom Templates subfolder from the C:\084361Data folder to the My Documents folder for the Administrator user.

16. Run Microsoft® Word 2003.

17. Set the security level for macros to Medium. (Choose Tools→Macro→Security. Select Medium and click OK.)

18. Open Automate Tasks from the My Documents folder. When prompted, enable the macros in Automate Tasks.

19. Choose Tools→Macro→Macros and click Organizer.

20. Select the NewMacros project and click Copy to copy it to the Normal template. Click Close. Close Automate Tasks and the Control Toolbox toolbar.

Before Every Class

1. Log on to the computer as the Administrator user.

2. Verify that the security level for macros is set to Medium. (Choose Tools→Macro→Security. Select Medium and click OK.)

3. Set the template location back to the default: with a blank document open, choose Tools→Options and select the File Locations tab. Select User Templates and click Modify. Enter or browse to select the path C:\Documents And Settings\Administrator\Application Data\Microsoft\Templates and click OK twice.

 You will need to have Windows folder view options set to show hidden files in order to browse for the path. If you turn on this option, turn it off again when you have completed Setup.

4. Close Microsoft® Word 2003.

5. Delete C:\Documents And Settings\Administrator\Application Data\Microsoft\Templates\ My Template.dot.

6. Delete C:\Documents And Settings\Administrator\Application Data\Microsoft\Templates\ Normal.dot.

7. Delete any existing data files and the Custom Templates subfolder from the Administrator user's My Documents folder. (Do not delete the default My Data Sources, My Music, or My Pictures subfolders.)

8. On the course CD-ROM, open the 084_361 folder. Then, open the Data folder. Run the 084361dd.exe self-extracting file located within. This will install a folder named 084361Data on your C drive. This folder contains all the data files that you will use to complete this course.

9. Move all the data files and the Custom Templates subfolder from the C:\084361Data folder to the My Documents folder for the Administrator user.

10. Run Microsoft® Word 2003. This will re-create the Normal.dot template in the default location with the default Microsoft® Word 2003 settings.

11. Open Automate Tasks from the My Documents folder. Enable the macros in Automate Tasks.

12. Choose Tools→Macro→Macros and click Organizer.

13. Select the NewMacros project and click Copy to copy it to the Normal template. Click Close. Close Automate Tasks.

14. If you do not have a physical printer, clear the print queue for your installed printer: Open the Printers or Printers And Faxes window, right-click the printer, and choose Cancel All Documents. Click Yes. Close the window.

List of Additional Files

Printed with each activity is a list of files students open to complete that activity. Many activities also require additional files that students do not open, but are needed to support the file(s) students are working with. These supporting files are included with the student data files on the course CD-ROM or data disk. Do not delete these files.

LESSON 1
Managing Lists

Lesson Objectives:

In this lesson, you will manage data in lists.

You will:

- Sort a list.
- Restart a numbered list.
- Create an outline numbered list.
- Customize list appearance.

Introduction

In this course, you will learn to add different customized document components to your Microsoft® Word 2003 documents. Because lists are such a common document element, customizing lists is a good place to start. In this lesson, you will manage lists in your Word documents.

The more you work with Word, the more you'll realize that lists are a useful way to present different types of information. But not all your lists will fit into simple, one-level bulleted or numbered formats. The more kinds of lists you create, the more you'll need to enhance the lists to create categories within the lists, show relationships between list items, and customize the list appearance to create an effective visual impact.

TOPIC A

Sort a List

When you create a list from scratch, the items will appear in order as you entered them. You might find later on that you need to rearrange the items by sorting this list. In this topic, you will sort lists of information.

There are several advantages to being able to sort a list in any order you choose. For one thing, it means that you don't have to worry about what order the items are in when you enter them, or what order you add items. For another, it means that you can show the information in your list in different ways depending on your different needs. Sorting your list helps you rearrange it in a logical order without the need for tedious cutting and pasting.

Sort Types

There are three different sort types you can use to sort information in lists in Word. For each type, you can sort in ascending or descending order.

Sort Type	Sort Rules	Sort Order
Text	First arranges items that begin with punctuation marks, then arranges items beginning with numbers, sorting on each individual digit (12 will sort before 2). Last arranges items that begin with letters.	• Ascending: A to Z • Descending: Z to A
Number	Ignores all characters except numbers, which can be anywhere in the list item. Sorts by numeric value (2 will sort before 12).	• Ascending: lowest to highest • Descending: highest to lowest

Sort Type	Sort Rules	Sort Order
Date	Sorts in chronological order. Recognizes dates and times formatted with standard time and date separator characters (hyphens, forward slashes, and so on).	• Ascending: earliest to most recent • Descending: most recent to earliest

Sort Fields

Definition:

A *sort field* is an individual item you can sort by within a paragraph in a list. Sort fields in a list paragraph are separated by a standard character. Word can use tabs, commas, or any specific character that you specify as the sort field separator. Sort fields enable you to perform multiple-level sorts on a list of items.

Example:

For example, if you have a list of names in the format "Smith, Mary," you have the option to sort by last name, then first name, breaking the ties between persons with the same last name.

Northeast Division

Comma (Field Separator)

- Smith, Sarah
- Smith, Jacob
- Jones, Arthur
- Jones, Dennis
- Smith, Mary
- Smith, Robert

Last Name Field   First Name Field

Figure 1-1: *A list of names.*

How to Sort a List

Procedure Reference: Sort a List

To sort a bullet list, numbered list, or series of paragraphs:

1. Select the list or series of paragraphs you want to sort.

2. Choose Table→Sort.

3. If you need to set sort options, click Options to open the Sort Options dialog box.
   - Select the sort field separator character if the sort field separator character for your list is different from the default separator character.

- Check Case Sensitive if you want to sort upper- and lower-case entries separately.
  - Select the sorting language if the language is different from the default.

4. Click OK to close the Sort Options dialog box.

5. From the first Sort By drop-down list, select the sort field you wish to sort by, if you are not sorting by paragraphs.

6. From the Type drop-down list, select the sort type (Text, Number, or Date).

7. Select Ascending or Descending.

8. Repeat the previous three steps for the Then By drop-down lists if you wish to sort by multiple sort fields.

9. From the My List Has area, select an option.
    - Select Header Row if you want the first paragraph of the list to stay as the first paragraph.
    - Select No Header Row if you want to sort all the selected paragraphs.

10. Click OK to perform the sort.

ACTIVITY 1-1

Sorting a List

Data Files:

- Burke List.doc

Setup:

You are logged on to the computer as Administrator. Word is running. The data files for this course are in the My Documents folder for the Administrator user.

Scenario:

You're a human resources manager for Burke Properties, Inc., a nationwide real estate and relocation firm. You're preparing a memo for the president of the company, Jan Burke, to inform her of the names of new agents that have been hired in various territories. You've entered the agents' names into a list in the order you received them from the hiring manager. However, the memo would be easier to read if the agents were listed by last name.

What You Do	How You Do It
1. **Open the Burke List memo document.**	a. Choose File→Open.
	b. From the Administrator user's My Documents folder, **select Burke List and click Open.**

2. **Sort the list.**

    a. In the body of the memo, **drag with the mouse to select all six bulleted paragraphs.**

    b. **Choose Table→Sort** to open the Sort Text dialog box.

    c. **Verify that the default sort order is an ascending text sort by paragraphs.**

    d. In the My List Has area, **verify that No Header Row is selected.**

    e. **Click OK** to sort the list by the agents' last names.

3. **Save the document as *My Burke List* and close the file.**

    a. **Choose File→Save As.**

    b. In the File Name text box, **type *My Burke List***

    c. **Click Save.**

    d. **Choose File→Close.**

ACTIVITY 1-2

Sorting a List by Sort Fields

Data Files:

- Burke Fields List.doc

Scenario:

You're a human resources manager for Burke Properties, Inc., a nationwide real estate and relocation firm. You're preparing a memo for the president of the company, Jan Burke, to inform her of the names of new agents that have been hired in various territories. You've entered the agents' names into a list in the memo in the order you received them from the hiring manager. There are two agents with the same last name. However, the memo would be easier to read if the agents were listed by last name, then by territory.

What You Do	How You Do It
1. Open the Burke Fields List memo document.	a. Choose File→Open.
	b. Select Burke Fields List and click Open.
2. Set the appropriate sort field separator code for the sort fields in the list.	a. On the Standard toolbar, **click the Toolbar Options button, and then click the Show/Hide button** ¶ to show non-printing characters.
	b. In this list, the agents' names and territories are separated by a tab character. In the body of the memo, **drag with the mouse to select all six bulleted paragraphs.**
	c. **Choose Table→Sort.**
	d. **Click Options** to open the Sort Options dialog box.

e. Under Separate Fields At, **select Tabs and click OK.**

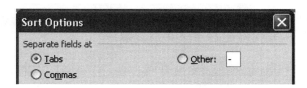

---

3. **Sort the list.**

a. From the Sort By drop-down list, **select Field 1** for an ascending text sort on Field 1.

b. From the Then By drop-down list, **select Field 2** for a secondary ascending text sort on Field 2.

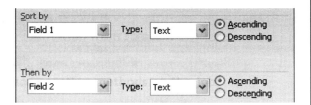

c. **Verify that No Header Row is selected and click OK** to sort the list by agents' last name, then territory.

---

4. **Save the document as *My Burke Fields List* and close the file.**

a. **Choose File→Save As.**

b. In the File Name text box, **type *My Burke Fields List***

c. **Click Save.**

d. **Choose File→Close.**

TOPIC B

Restart a List

In this lesson, you will manage a variety of lists. One type of list you might encounter is a list that stops and then starts again. In this topic, you will restart a list.

Have you ever seen a case where a list was interrupted with some other information? Maybe it's a numbered list that gives step-by-step instructions for something, and there's a little bit of commentary about one of the items. That extra paragraph or two isn't another step in the list and it shouldn't be numbered. Restarting a list lets you handle this type of situation; you can turn off the numbers or bullets, insert your comment, and pick up the list again right where you left off.

How to Continue a Numbered List

Procedure Reference: Continue a Numbered List as You Type

To continue a numbered list as you type:

1. On the Formatting toolbar, click the Numbering button.

2. Enter the items for the first portion of the list.

3. Turn off numbering:
   - Press Enter twice, or
   - Press Enter once and click the Numbering button to turn off numbering.

4. Enter the paragraphs that do not need numbers.

5. Press Enter to start a new paragraph.

6. Choose Format→Bullets And Numbering.

7. Select a numbering style if none is selected.

8. Select Continue Previous List and click OK.

 To continue a list with the previous numbering style, you can right-click the new item and choose Continue Numbering, or choose Continue Numbering from the list SmartTag.

9. Enter the remaining items in the list.

Procedure Reference: Continue Numbering in an Existing List

To continue numbering in an existing list:

1. Select the portion of the list that does not need numbers.

2. Click the Numbering button to turn off numbering for that portion of the list. Numbering will automatically continue in the remaining paragraphs of the list.

Restarting a List

You can start renumbering any item in a list as number 1 by right-clicking the item and choosing Restart Numbering.

ACTIVITY 1-3

Continuing a Numbered List

Data Files:

- Burke Numbered List.doc

Scenario:

As the human resources manager for Burke Properties, you need to create a memo informing hiring managers of the steps they need to take when hiring new employees. You've created part of the memo, including the first five items in the list. Now, you want to add a comment to the last item that you entered, but that comment isn't part of the list of procedures. Then you need to add a final item to the list.

With·all·the·new·hiring·at·our·firm,·I·wanted·to·inform·all·hiring·managers·about·the·proper· procedures·to·follow·after·hiring·a·new·employee:·¶

1.→ When·the·new·employee·is·selected,·forward·the·employee's·application·to·Human· Resources,·along·with·the·Notice·of·New·Hire·form·(available·from·HR).·HR·will· issue·an·official·offer·letter.¶

2.→ HR·will·inform·you·when·the·employee·has·accepted·the·offer.·¶

3.→ Contact·the·employee·to·verify·the·employee's·start·date·and·work·hours.¶

4.→ Contact·Facilities·to·arrange·for·desk·space,·computer,·and·telephone·access·for·the· new·employee.¶

5.→ Create·an·agenda·for·the·employee's·first·day.·¶

Let·me·know·if·there·is·any·more·information·that·you·need!¶

Figure 1-2: *The original list.*

With·all·the·new·hiring·at·our·firm,·I·wanted·to·inform·all·hiring·managers·about·the·proper· procedures·to·follow·after·hiring·a·new·employee:·¶

1.→ When·the·new·employee·is·selected,·forward·the·employee's·application·to·Human· Resources,·along·with·the·Notice·of·New·Hire·form·(available·from·HR).·HR·will· issue·an·official·offer·letter.¶

2.→ HR·will·inform·you·when·the·employee·has·accepted·the·offer.·¶

3.→ Contact·the·employee·to·verify·the·employee's·start·date·and·work·hours.¶

4.→ Contact·Facilities·to·arrange·for·desk·space,·computer,·and·telephone·access·for·the· new·employee.¶

5.→ Create·an·agenda·for·the·employee's·first·day.¶

Note:·Include·an·HR·orientation·session·in·the·agenda.¶

6.→ Please·greet·the·new·employee·at·the·door·on·the·first·day.¶

Let·me·know·if·there·is·any·more·information·that·you·need!¶

Figure 1-3: *The completed list.*

What You Do	How You Do It
1. **Add commentary text to the end of the numbered list in the Burke Numbered List memo.**	a. **Open Burke Numbered List.**
	b. **Place the insertion point at the end of item 5 in the list.**
	c. **Press Enter** to add a new paragraph numbered as item 6.
	d. On the Formatting toolbar, **click the Numbering button** 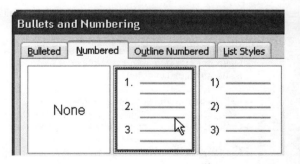 to turn off numbering.
	e. **Press Tab** to align the new paragraph with the list items.
	f. **Type** *Note: Include an HR orientation session in the agenda.*
2. **Complete the numbered list.**	a. **Press Enter** to add another unnumbered paragraph.
	b. **Choose Format→Bullets And Numbering.**
	c. **Select the Numbered tab.**
	d. **Select the first numbering option,** to the right of the None option.
	e. **Select Continue Previous List and click OK** to number the paragraph as item 6.
	f. **Type** *Please greet the new employee at the door on the first day.*

3. Save the document as *My Burke Numbered List* and close the file.

a. Save the document as *My Burke Numbered List*

b. Close the file.

TOPIC C

Create an Outline Numbered List

So far in this lesson, you have worked with simple bulleted and numbered lists. Another type of list you might need to create is an outline numbered list. In this topic, you will create an outline numbered list.

Outline numbered lists are handy any time you have multiple levels of information in your list. Outlines are just one example of this type of list; you also might have a set of step-by-step instructions with substeps, or a list of various topic headings with bullet points for each topic. Outline numbered lists provide you with lots of options so that you can structure your list around more complex types of information.

Outline Numbered Lists

Definition:

An *outline numbered list* is a list with a hierarchical structure. Items on lower levels are demoted, by indenting, to distinguish them from items on higher levels. The number or bullet format is configured separately for each level of the list. For example, the list can mix numbers on some levels with bullets on other levels.

Example:

This list has items on two levels. The first level uses numbers, and the second level uses bullets.

Northeast Division Spring Training Program

1. **Meet and Greet**
    *   Check in
    *   Breakfast
2. **Sales Manager Presentation**
    *   First Quarter Results
    *   Revised Territories

Figure 1-4: *An outline numbered list.*

How to Create an Outline Numbered List

Procedure Reference: Apply an Outline Numbered List Format

To apply an outline numbered list format to an existing list:

1. Select the list.

2. Open the Bullets And Numbering dialog box.

3. Select the Outline Numbered tab.

4. Select a list style and click OK.

5. Demote and promote items as necessary:
   - Press Tab to indent and demote items, and press Shift+Tab to outdent and promote items, or
   - Click the Increase Indent or Decrease Indent buttons on the Formatting toolbar to demote and promote items, respectively.

6. Enter additional list items as necessary.

Procedure Reference: Create an Outline Numbered List

To create an outline numbered list as you type:

1. Open the Bullets And Numbering dialog box:
   - Choose Format→Bullets And Numbering, or
   - Right-click and choose Bullets And Numbering.

2. Select the Outline Numbered tab.

3. Select a list style and click OK.

4. Enter the list. Demote and promote items as necessary:
   - Press Tab to indent and demote items, and press Shift+Tab to outdent and promote items, or
   - Click the Increase Indent or Decrease Indent buttons on the Formatting toolbar to demote and promote items, respectively.

5. At the end of the list, discontinue the outline numbered list.
   - Press Enter twice, or
   - Press Enter once, and then click the Numbering button on the Formatting toolbar.

Converting an Existing Numbered List

You can convert items in a numbered list to outline number list format simply by demoting entries in the list. Word will automatically apply an outline numbered list format to the new subordinate step.

ACTIVITY 1-4

Creating an Outline Numbered List

Data Files:

- Report Outline.doc

Scenario:

Jan Burke, the president of Burke Properties, has asked you to create a draft of the annual Stockholder Report for the company. You've begun to draft a list of the main points that you will need to cover in the report, and you plan to add a few more items and present it to Jan for her approval. You realize it will be easier for Jan to read if you present it in an outline format, rather than as a one-level list.

What You Do	How You Do It
1. Apply an outline numbered list format to the **Report Outline** document.	a. **Open Report Outline.**
	b. **Drag to select all the text in the list, from the "President's Message" item through "New relocation team."**
	c. **Right-click the list and choose Bullets And Numbering.**
	d. **Select the Outline Numbered tab.**
	e. **Select the first outline numbered list style,** to the right of the None option.
	f. **Click OK** to number all items in the list at the first level.

2. **Demote the subordinate items below each main section.** (The main section headings appear in bold.)

a. **Position the insertion point at the beginning of the line that reads "This year's accomplishments."**

b. **Press Tab** to demote the item and display it with a lower-case letter heading.

c. **Position the insertion point at the beginning of the "Next Year's Goals" line.**

d. **Press Tab** to Demote the "Next year's goals" line.

e. **Demote the "Departmental reorganization" and "New relocation team" lines.**

3. **Add two manager's names, Pat Markus and Daniel Ortiz, as subordinate items to "New relocation team."**

a. **Position the insertion point at the end of the "New relocation team" line.**

b. **Press Enter** to add a new paragraph.

c. **Press Tab** to demote the new paragraph another level.

d. The new paragraph appears with a lower-case Roman numeral. **Type** *Pat Markus* **and press Enter.**

e. **Type** *Daniel Ortiz*

Stockholder·Annual·Report¶

·Draft·Outline¶

¶

1)→**President's·Message¶**

   a → This·year's·accomplishments¶

   b → Next·year's·goals¶

2)→**Organizational·Growth¶**

   a → Departmental·reorganization¶

   b → New·relocation·team¶

     i)→ Pat·Markus¶

     ii)→ Daniel·Ortiz¶

4. **Save the document as** *My Outline* **and close the document.**

a. **Save the document as** *My Outline*

b. **Close the file.**

TOPIC D

Customize List Appearance

After completing the first topics in this lesson, you now can create and structure all different types of lists. Another way to manage lists is to change their appearance. In this topic, you will customize the appearance of your lists.

As you know, Word provides a number of built-in list formats for each different type of list, and one of those formats might be just right for you. However, maybe your list needs an option that's just a little bit different from the ones on the menu. Maybe you need to combine bullets and numbers within your list; maybe you need to tighten up the spacing on the list to fit more information on each line; maybe you need to call more attention to certain parts of the list. Word gives you the tools you need to customize every aspect of the list's appearance.

List Appearance Options

There are a variety of options you can configure to customize the appearance of your list. The options include such characteristics as bullet style, number style, bullet or number position, and text position. The specific options available vary depending upon the list type. See Table 1-1 for a description of the options that you can apply to different types of lists.

List Appearance Options

Table 1-1: *List Appearance Options*

Option	Available in These List Types	Controls
Bullet Character	Bullet List	The symbol or picture used as the bullet, and the font from which the bullet is selected.
Bullet Position	Bullet List	The distance of the bullet from the left margin.
Text Position	Bullet List, Numbered List, Outline Numbered List	The amount the text is indented. Tab Space After controls the amount of space between the bullet or number and the first line of text in the list item. Indent At controls the amount of space between the bullet or number and the subsequent lines of text in the list item.
Number Format	Numbered List, Outline Numbered List	The style of numbering (Arabic numerals, Roman numerals, letters, and so on) and the font from which the numbers are selected.
Number Position	Numbered List, Outline Numbered List	The amount the number is indented from the left margin, and whether the number is aligned left, center, or right at this point.

There are some additional, advanced formatting options available for outline numbered lists. For example, you can automatically apply styles to specific levels of the list. See the Microsoft Office Word Help system for more information on these advanced options.

How to Customize List Appearance

Procedure Reference: Customize List Appearance

To customize list appearance:

1. Select the list items you want to customize if you have already entered them.

2. Choose Format→Bullets And Numbering, or right-click the selection and choose Bullets And Numbering.

3. Select the tab in the dialog box that corresponds to the type of list you are customizing (Bulleted, Numbered, or Outline Numbered).

4. To change the list format to another existing format, click the list format you want.

5. To apply custom formatting, click Customize.

    a. For an outline numbered list, select the level of the list you want to customize.

    b. Select the customization options you want.

    c. For an outline numbered list, repeat the previous two steps for other levels of the list you wish to customize.

    d. Click OK to close the Customize dialog box.

6. Enter any list items you have not already entered.

Procedure Reference: Create a Custom Bullet

To create custom bullet characters for bulleted lists or for bulleted levels in outline numbered lists:

1. Open the Customize dialog box for your bulleted list.

2. Click Font if you want to change the font you are choosing your bullet from.

3. Select a bullet character.

    - For a bulleted list:
        — Click Bullet to select a different bullet symbol from those available in the current font, or
        — Click Picture to select a picture file to use as a bullet.
    - For an outline numbered list:
        — Select New Bullet from the Number Style drop-down list to select a different bullet symbol from those available in the current font, or
        — Select New Picture from the Number Style drop-down list to select a picture file to use as a bullet.

4. Click OK to close all open dialog boxes.

ACTIVITY 1-5

Customizing a List

Data Files:

- Burke Custom List.doc

Scenario:

You've created a memo to inform managers of the procedures to follow when hiring a new employee. There is an outline list in the memo that documents the various steps the managers need to take. As you review the list, you realize that the steps at the second level of the list are numbered, but they are not really sequential.

What You Do	How You Do It
1. Customize the list in Burke Custom List so that the subordinate steps in the list appear with bullets rather than numbers.	a. **Open Burke Custom List.** b. In the body of the memo, **drag with the mouse to select list item 1 through list item 5e** in the outline list. c. **Choose Format→Bullets And Numbering.** d. On the Outline Numbered tab of the dialog box, **click Customize.** e. In the Number Format area, in the Level list, **select 2.** 

f. From the Number Style drop-down list, select the first round bullet character.

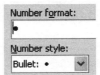

g. **Click OK** to format the subordinate steps with bullets rather than letters.

2. **Save the document as *My Custom List* and close the file.**

a. **Save the document as *My Custom List***

b. **Close the document.**

Lesson 1 Follow-up

In this lesson, you customized and managed a variety of lists in Word documents. Because lists are such a common element in documents, knowing how to customize and enhance them will help you organize and present your list information in the most effective way.

1. **What types of lists have you seen in the business documents you work with?**

2. **How will Word's list-management features help you?**

LESSON 2

Customizing Tables and Charts

Lesson Objectives:

In this lesson, you will customize tables and charts.

You will:

- Sort a table.
- Modify table structure.
- Merge or split cells.
- Position text in a table cell.
- Apply borders and shading.
- Perform calculations in a table.
- Create a chart from a Word table.
- Modify a chart.

Introduction

In Lesson 1, you managed and customized lists in your Word documents. Word tables are closely related to lists because you can use tables to present some of the same kinds of information. In addition, you can use Word tables as the basis for creating custom charts in your Word documents. In this lesson, you will customize tables and charts.

You know how to create a great-looking basic table very quickly. But you'll often find that modifications to the structure and appearance of your basic tables can help you communicate with your readers more effectively. From creating a great-looking header for your table, to changing the arrangement of the columns and rows, to displaying your table information as a chart in your document, customizing your tables enables you to create the exact results that you need.

TOPIC A

Sort a Table

In this lesson, you'll be customizing Word tables. One of the simplest ways to do so is to sort the items you've entered into the table. In this topic, you'll sort the rows in a table.

Sorting your table has the same advantages as sorting a list: you don't have to worry about the order of the items as you're entering them, and you can change the order of the table as needed without having to cut and paste information from one place to another. Whether you need to show a table of employee information in alphabetical order, or a table of sales figures in numeric order, sorting your table enables you to display the information in the way that best suits your needs.

How to Sort a Table

Procedure Reference: Sort a Table

Sorting a table is similar to sorting a list. To sort a table:

1. Select the portion of the table you want to sort.
   - Select the entire table, including the first row, if the first row has column headings you want to use to identify the sort order.
   - Select only the rows in the table that contain data if you want to sort by fields within one of the table columns.

2. Choose Table→Sort.

3. Click Options to open the Sort Options dialog box if you need to set sort options.
   - Select the field separator character if you are sorting by fields within a column, and the field separator character for the column you want to sort by is different from the default separator character.
   - Check Case Sensitive if you want to sort upper- and lower-case entries separately.
   - Select the sorting language if the language is different from the default.

4. Click OK to close the Sort Options dialog box.

5. From the first Sort By drop-down list, select the first column you wish to sort by.

6. From the first Using drop-down list, select the field within the column that you are sorting by, if needed.

7. From the Type drop-down list, select the sort type (Text, Number, or Date).

8. Select Ascending or Descending.

9. Repeat the previous four steps for the Then By drop-down lists if you wish to sort by multiple columns.

10. From the My List Has area, select an option.
    *   Select Header Row if you want the first row you selected to remain as the first row.
    *   Select No Header Row if you want to sort all the selected rows.

11. Click OK to perform the sort.

Table Selection Techniques

You can use various techniques to select areas in a table.

To Select This	Do This
The entire table	• Click in the table and choose Table→Select→Table. • Click the square move handle in the upper-right corner of the table. The mouse will be a four-way arrow.
A row	• Click in the row and choose Table→Select→Row. • Click in the margin just to the left of the row. The mouse will be a right-pointing arrow.
A column	• Click in the column and choose Table→Select→Column. • Click the gridline at the top of the column. The mouse will be a dark, down-pointing arrow.
Several rows	• Drag in the margin just to the left of the rows.
Several columns	• Drag along the gridline just above the columns.
A single cell (This is rarely required. It is normally sufficient to click in a cell to activate it.)	• Click in the cell and choose Table→Select→Cell. • Click in the lower-left corner of the cell. The mouse will be a dark, right-pointing arrow.
A group of cells	• Click in a cell, hold Shift, and press the arrow keys. • Drag over the cells.

ACTIVITY 2-1

Sorting a Table

Data Files:

- Mortgage Letter.doc

Scenario:

You're preparing a letter for a real estate client who has inquired about comparative mortgage loan rates. The letter includes a table of loan rates. The first row of the table contains descriptive column headings. After drafting the letter, you realize that the client will probably want the information listed alphabetically by city.

What You Do	How You Do It
1. Sort the loan rates table in the Mortgage Letter document and save it as *My Mortgage Letter*.	a. **Open Mortgage Letter.**
	b. **Click in the Location cell in the table and choose Table→Select→Table to select the table.**
	c. **Choose Table→Sort.**
	d. **Verify that you will sort alphabetically by the Location column and that Header Row is selected.**

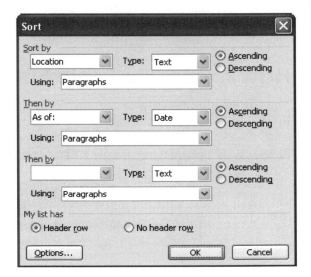

e. **Click OK** to sort the table.

f. **Save the document as *My Mortgage Letter***

Topic B

Modify Table Structure

There are a variety of ways to customize a basic table. One of the things you might need to do is to alter the structure of a table after you've created it. In this topic, you'll modify the structure of tables.

Imagine this scenario: you've created a table for the third-quarter report that shows the year-to-date revenues for your territory. Then, your manager decides it would be best to include a full year's worth of data, and compare it to the same data for another territory. You're going to need extra columns and rows, and you might even need to move some of the existing information. You could start from scratch and create a whole new table structure, but then you would have to re-enter all your existing information. Why bother? Take your existing table and modify its structure to meet the new requirements.

How to Modify Table Structure

You can modify the structure of a table by inserting, deleting, or moving columns or rows, or by changing the column width or row height.

Procedure Reference: Insert or Delete Columns or Rows

To insert or delete columns or rows:

1. Select the appropriate items in the table:
    - If you are inserting or deleting a single column or row, place the insertion point in an adjacent column or row.
    - If you are inserting or deleting multiple columns or rows, select the number of columns or rows in the table equal to the number you want to insert or delete.

2. Insert or delete the columns or rows:
    - To insert, choose Table→Insert and then select the appropriate option:
        — Columns To The Left
        — Columns To The Right
        — Rows Above
        — Rows Below
    - To delete, choose Table→Delete→Columns or Table→Delete→Rows.

Alternate Methods for Inserting or Deleting Columns and Rows

You can insert columns and rows by selecting the appropriate option from the Insert Table drop-down list on the Tables And Borders toolbar. You can also insert or delete columns or rows by right-clicking the selected columns or rows and choosing the appropriate option from the shortcut menu. If you insert by using this method, rows are inserted above the current row, and columns are inserted to the right of the current column.

Inserting or Deleting Cells

You can insert individual cells by choosing Table→Insert→Cells from the menu, or by choosing Insert Cells from the Insert Table drop-down list on the Tables And Borders toolbar. When you do so, you can shift the existing cells down in the current columns or to the right in the current rows.

You can delete individual cells by choosing Table→Delete→Cells. When you do so, you can shift the existing cells up in the current columns or to the left in the current rows.

Procedure Reference: Move Columns or Rows

To move columns or rows:

1. Select the appropriate items in the table:
   - If you are moving a single column or row, place the insertion point in the column or row.
   - If you are moving multiple columns or rows, select the columns or rows.

2. Cut the columns or rows:
   - Choose Edit→Cut, or
   - Right-click the selection and choose Cut, or
   - Click the Cut button on the Standard toolbar.

3. Place the insertion point in the row below the new row location, or in the column to the left of the new column location.

4. Paste the rows or columns:
   - Choose Edit→Paste Columns, or
   - Choose Edit→Paste Rows.

Cutting and Pasting Cells

You cannot move individual cells by cutting and pasting. When you paste cells, Word replaces the contents of the target cells.

Procedure Reference: Set Column Width or Row Height by Using Table Boundaries

To set the column width or row height by using the table boundaries:

1. Place the mouse pointer on the boundary to the right of the column you wish to adjust or below the row you wish to adjust, so that the mouse pointer becomes a double-headed arrow (this: ┼║┼ or this: ⊟).

2. Set the column width or row height:
   - Drag the border up, down, right, or left to set an approximate size value.
   - Double-click the border to automatically adjust the size to fit the row or column contents.

Procedure Reference: Set Column Width or Row Height to a Specific Value

To set column width or row height to a specific value:

1. Place the insertion point inside the table. If you want to set the value for more than one row or column at the same time, select the rows or columns.

2. Choose Table→Table Properties.

3. Select the Row or Column tab.

4. Click the Previous or Next buttons to select the column or row you wish to affect.

5. For rows, check Specify Height.

6. Enter the value you want for rows or columns:
   - Enter the value on the Row tab in the Specify Height area.
   - Enter the value on the Column tab in the Preferred Width area.

7. Click the Previous or Next buttons if you need to set values for additional rows or columns.

8. Set the values for the additional rows or columns.

9. When you have finished, click OK.

ACTIVITY 2-2

Modifying Table Structure

Setup:
My Mortgage Letter is open.

Scenario:
As you are preparing your mortgage rates letter, the client calls and reminds you that the company he works for is opening a branch office in Rochester, NY later in the year, and he might possibly be transferred to that location. He would like you to include specific information on loan rates for Rochester. Rates in Rochester were set at 6.13% on July 8. You also realize that the rate percentage is more important information to your customer than the effective date. The table also seems to have too much white space in each column.

What You Do	How You Do It
1. **Insert the additional row of information in My Mortgage Letter.**	a. **Click in the cell that reads Seattle, WA.**
	b. **Choose Table→Insert→Rows Above.**
	c. **In the first cell in the new row, type *Rochester, NY***
	d. **In the second cell in the new row, type *July 8, 2003***
	e. **In the last cell in the new row, type *6.13***

2. **How else could you get the new row into the correct location in the table?**

3. **Reverse the Rate and As Of columns.**

    a. **Click in the Rate cell and choose Table→ Select→Column** to select the Rate column.

    b. **Choose Edit→Cut.**

    c. **Verify that the insertion point is in the As Of column and choose Edit→Paste Columns.**

    d. **Click in the Rate cell** to deselect the column.

4. **Adjust the column widths to fit the column contents.**

    a. **Place the mouse pointer anywhere on the border line to the right of the Location column.** The mouse pointer should become a double-headed arrow.

    b. **Double-click the border** to adjust the column width automatically to fit the column's contents.

    c. **Double-click the border to the right of the Rate column** to adjust its width.

    d. **Double-click the border to the right of the As Of column** to adjust its width.

    e. **Save the document.**

TOPIC C

Merge or Split Cells

In Topic 2B, you modified the structure of a table by altering the configuration of the table's columns and rows. It's also possible to change the configuration of individual cells in the table. In this topic, you will merge or split table cells.

Merging and splitting cells is useful when you want a table that's not a plain grid structure. Imagine a table with a title in a single big cell that spans the width of all the other columns. Or a label cell that runs vertically down the side of the table. Or a cell entry that needs to be broken up into two sections. Merging and splitting cells lets you manage the cell shape and placement in situations like these.

Cell Merge and Cell Split

There are two methods for altering the configuration of specific groups of cells in a table: *cell merge* and *cell split*.

- Cell merge enables you to take a group of adjacent cells and combine them into a single, larger cell. The new cell will be the size and shape of the original selection.

- Cell split enables you to divide a single cell into a group of adjacent cells. You can split the cell into a specified number of columns or rows that take up the same amount of space as the original cell.

Project Manager Assignments	
Project Code Name	Project Manager
Atlas	Jim Simpson
Midas	Judy Rodriguez
Cassandra	Marilyn Beck (Phase1)
	Jim Simpson (Phase 2)

Figure 2-1: *Merged and split cells.*

Splitting Multiple Cells

You can also split multiple cells. If you do this, you have the option to merge the cells together first before splitting them into a different arrangement.

How to Merge or Split Cells

Procedure Reference: Merge Cells

To merge multiple adjacent cells into a single table cell:

1. Select the adjacent cells you want to merge together.

2. Merge the cells:
   - Choose Table→Merge Cells.
   - Right-click the selected cells and choose Merge Cells.
   - Click the Merge Cells button on the Tables And Borders toolbar.

Merging Cells Containing Content

If you merge several cells that contain content, the information in the first cell will appear as the first paragraph in the merged cell, the information in the second cell will appear as the second paragraph in the merged cell, and so on.

Procedure Reference: Split Cells

To split a table cell into multiple cells:

1. Place the insertion point in the cell you want to split.

2. Display the Split Cells dialog box:
   - Choose Table→Split Cells.
   - Right-click the selected cells and choose Split Cells.
   - Click the Split Cells button on the Tables And Borders toolbar.

3. Enter the number of columns and rows you want to split the cell into and click OK.

Splitting a Table

You can also split a table into two separate tables by choosing Table→Split Table.

ACTIVITY **2-3**

Merging Cells

Setup:

My Mortgage Letter is open.

Scenario:

Looking at your mortgage rates table, you realize that you could use your introductory paragraph (30-year fixed-rate mortgage loan rates) as a title row within the table. However, the text is too long to fit in a single table cell at the current cell width.

What You Do	How You Do It
1. **Insert a new blank row for the title row in My Mortgage Letter.**	a. **Click in the Location cell** to position the insertion point in the first row in the table.
	b. **Choose Table→Insert→Rows Above** to insert the new row with all the cells selected.

2. **Merge the cells in the new title row.**

   a. **With all the cells in the new row selected, choose Table→Merge Cells** to merge the row into one single large cell.

   b. **Click in the Location cell** to deselect the header row.

3. **Move the text into the new title row.**

   a. **Select the text that reads 30-year fixed-rate mortgage loan rates.**

 You do not need to select the paragraph mark that follows the text, but it is all right to do so. You can click at the beginning of the line, then hold Shift and click at the end of the line to select the precise amount of text.

   b. **Choose Edit→Cut.**

   c. **Click in the header row in the table.**

   d. **Choose Edit→Paste.**

 You can also drag the selected text into the cell to move it.

   e. **Save the document.**

TOPIC D

Position Text in a Table Cell

In Topic 2C, you merged cells within a table. Once you've adjusted the structure of the cells, you might find that you need to alter the placement of the text within those cells, or within other cells in the table. In this topic, you'll position text in a table cell.

Now you know that you can make a cell any size and shape that you need. But what about the information in that cell? You don't want a wide header cell with all the text crowded in one corner. It would look best if the text in a cell matched the general structure of the cell. You can alter the text to suit the cell appearance you need by adjusting the text position.

How to Position Text in a Table Cell

You can position text in a table cell by changing the text direction or the cell alignment.

Procedure Reference: Change Cell Alignment

To change the alignment of text in cells:

1. Select the cells.

2. Set the alignment:

    - Right-click the cells, choose Cell Alignment, and select one of the nine options.

    - Select one of the nine options from the Align drop-down list on the Tables and Borders toolbar (the default is Top Left).

Procedure Reference: Change Text Direction

To change the text direction of cells:

1. Select the cells.

2. Set the text direction:

    - Right-click the selected cells, choose Text Direction, and select an orientation (horizontal, vertical up, or vertical down). Click OK.

    - Click the Change Text Direction button on the Tables And Borders toolbar to cycle through the three orientation settings.

    The height of the cells will change automatically to accommodate vertical orientation.

ACTIVITY 2-4

Positioning Text in a Table Cell

Setup:
My Mortgage Letter is open. A header row has been added.

Scenario:
You feel that the header row of your new table needs to stand out more. You can change the height of the cell, but then you'll have to see if the text still looks balanced in the cell.

What You Do	How You Do It
1. Increase the row height for the header row in the table in My Mortgage Letter.	a. Position the insertion point in the first row of the table.
	b. Choose Table→Table Properties and select the Row tab.
	c. Verify that Row 1 appears in the Size area and check Specify Height.

d. In the Specify Height text box, **type *0.5***

e. **Click OK.**

---

2. **Center the text in the header row.**

a. **Right-click the header row cell** to open the shortcut menu.

b. **Point to Cell Alignment and click the middle option** to center the text horizontally and vertically in the cell.

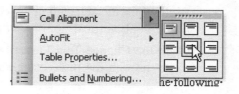

c. **Save the document.**

Topic E

Apply Borders and Shading

When you build a basic table, it's simple to format it using Word's built-in AutoFormat settings. However, you can also customize the table formatting by modifying the table's borders and shading properties manually. In this topic, you'll apply custom borders and shading to tables.

Word's AutoFormat choices give you a great, quick way to apply table formats such as borders and shading. But there might be cases where you can't get the effect you want from an AutoFormat. Maybe you need shading and border colors that match your company's letterhead; maybe you need to modify the shading for better print output. Whatever the reason, you can apply your own borders and shading for ultimate control of the appearance of your table.

Borders and Shading Options

You can draw borders around or through the cells in selected parts of a table. See Table 2-1 for a list and description of the table border options. You can apply grayscale or colored shading to cells in selected parts of a table. See Table 2-2 for a list and description of the table shading options.

Borders and Shading Options

Table 2-1: *Table Border Options*

Table Border Option	Controls
Setting	Which sides of the cells will have borders and whether cells have diagonal lines through them. The available choices vary depending on whether you apply borders to individual cells or the whole table.
Style	The appearance of the border line: single, double, dashed, and so on.
Color	The color of the border line.
Width	The width of the border line.

Table 2-2: *Table Shading Options*

Table Shading Option	Controls
Fill Color	The fill color for the shading.
Pattern Style	Whether the fill is applied as a grayscale percentage, or as a pattern alternating the fill color and black.
Pattern Color	The alternate color in a pattern; for example, you can have a stripe pattern in two separate colors instead of the fill color and black.

Changing Table Fonts

You can also alter the appearance of a table by modifying the fonts in the table. Simply select the text and use standard font-formatting techniques.

How to Apply Borders and Shading

Procedure Reference: Apply Borders and Shading with the Borders And Shading Dialog Box

To apply borders and shading by using the Borders And Shading dialog box:

1. Select the table or table cells that you want to format.

2. Choose Format→Borders And Shading, or right-click the selection and choose Borders And Shading.

3. On the Borders tab, select the settings you want for your borders. You can see how your choices will look in the Preview box.

4. On the Borders tab, from the Apply To drop-down list, select Cell to apply the formats to just the selected cell, or Table to apply them to the entire table.

5. On the Shading tab, select the shading options you want. You can see how your choices will look in the Preview box.

6. On the Shading tab, from the Apply To drop-down list, select Cell to apply the formats to just the selected cell, or select Table to apply them to the entire table.

7. Click OK.

Procedure Reference: Apply Borders and Shading with the Toolbar

To apply borders and shading by using the Tables And Borders toolbar:

1. Select the table or table cells you want to format.

2. Display the Tables And Borders toolbar.

3. On the Tables And Borders toolbar, select the formatting options you want to apply:

    - Click the Line Style drop-down arrow and select a line style.
    - Click the Line Weight drop-down arrow and select a line weight.
    - Click the Border Color drop-down arrow and select a border color.
    - Click the Borders drop-down arrow and specify the cell borders.
    - Click the Shading Color drop-down arrow and select a shading fill color.

ACTIVITY 2-5

Applying Borders and Shading

Setup:

My Mortgage Letter is open.

Scenario:

Because your client is particularly interested in the information for Rochester, NY, you want to highlight that row of information in the table to call attention to it.

What You Do	How You Do It
1. Apply a double-line border to the Rochester, NY row in the table in My Mortgage Letter.	**a. Select the Rochester, NY row.** **b. Right-click the row and choose Borders And Shading.** **c. On the Borders tab, in the Setting area, click Box.**

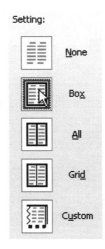

	d. In the Style list, select the double-line style.

	e. Verify that Cell appears in the Apply To box and click OK to apply the border to the selected row.
2. Apply pale blue shading to the Rochester, NY row in the table.	**a. With the row still selected, right-click the row and choose Borders And Shading.** **b. Select the Shading tab.**

c. In the Fill area, **select the Pale Blue fill color on the bottom row.**

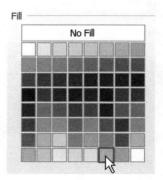

d. **Verify that Cell appears in the Apply To box and click OK** to apply the shading to the selected row.

e. To view the new formatting, **click in the Seattle, WA cell** to deselect the row.

f. **Save and close the document.**

TOPIC F

Perform Calculations in a Table

Many Word tables that you will construct will contain numeric information as well as text. Microsoft Word enables you to perform simple calculations on numeric information in tables. In this topic, you'll perform calculations in a table.

Word processing is mostly about words, but once you start putting numbers in tables, it starts to be a little bit about math, too. You just can't get the most of your numbers without doing a little math on them, whether the calculations are totals, averages, or simple addition and subtraction. You can use calculations in your tables to help you get the most out of any numeric information.

Formulas in Word Tables

Definition:

A formula in a Word table is a set of codes in a table cell that instructs Word to perform mathematical calculations. The result of the formula's mathematical operation appears in the table cell that contains the formula. A table formula consists of two parts: a *function,* which is the mathematical operator, and one or more *arguments,* which are the numbers to calculate.

Word table formulas are intended for simple, one-time calculations on small groups of numbers in a table. If you need to perform more complex calculations, use a dedicated spreadsheet application such as Microsoft® Office Excel 2003.

Example:

The =SUM function performs addition on the provided arguments. =SUM is commonly used in tables to create totals. For example, the function =SUM(100,200) would display the value 300 in a table cell.

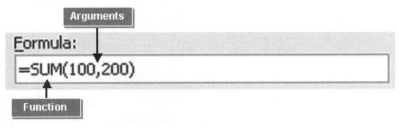

Figure 2-2: *A =SUM function.*

Common Functions

There are a variety of functions you can enter in a table formula. Functions begin with an equals sign (=). Each function performs different operations on the provided arguments. Besides the =SUM function, other common functions include =AVERAGE, to return an average of the arguments, and =PRODUCT, to multiply the arguments together. For a complete list and description of the functions that Word table formulas can accept, see the Microsoft Office Word Help system.

Arguments

Formula arguments are enclosed in parentheses and separated by commas. You can include any of the following as valid arguments in a table formula:

- Numbers.
- Names of adjacent groups of cells. The name describes the position of the cells in relation to the formula cell. For example, the (LEFT) argument refers to all the cells that contain numbers that are to the left of the formula cell.
- Table references. Table references assign a grid letter and number to each cell in the table. The columns are assigned letters from left to right, the rows are assigned numbers from top to bottom. See Table 2-3 for an example of how table references are assigned.

Table 2-3: *Cell References in a Word Table*

A1	B1	C1	D1
A2	B2	C2	D2
A3	B3	C3	D3
A4	B4	C4	D4

How To Perform Calculations in a Table

Procedure Reference: Use AutoSum

Because calculating totals is so common, there is a button on the toolbar that you can use to create a total formula quickly. To use the AutoSum button to create a total formula:

1. Display the Tables And Borders toolbar.

2. Place the insertion point in the cell that will contain the calculation result.

3. Click the AutoSum button.

AutoSum Guidelines

Keep the following points in mind if you use the AutoSum button:

- AutoSum defaults to =SUM(ABOVE), unless there are no numbers in the cells above the calculation, in which case AutoSum will perform a =SUM(LEFT).

- You cannot select a number format when you use AutoSum.

Procedure Reference: Enter Formulas in a Table

To enter a specific formula in a table:

1. Place the insertion point in the cell that will contain the calculation result.

2. Choose Table→Formula.

3. Enter the formula. If you are entering a function, you can type the function in, or you can select it from the Paste Function drop-down list.

4. Choose a number format if you need a format other than the default. (By default, the format of the calculation result will match the format of the numbers used in the calculation.)

5. Click OK.

Default Formula Entries

When you choose Table→Formula, the Formula text box will typically default to =SUM(ABOVE) if there are any numbers in the cells above the formula cell. If there are no numbers in the cells above the formula cell, the formula will default to =SUM(LEFT). To enter a different formula, delete the =SUM function from the Formula text box.

Updating Formulas

The results of table formulas do not automatically update when other numbers in the table change. To update the results of a formula, place the insertion point in the cell that contains the formula and press F9.

ACTIVITY 2-6

Performing Calculations in a Table

Data Files:

- Loan Rates.doc

Scenario:

You are creating an information sheet to send to customers to illustrate how affordable home improvement loans can be. You've created a table showing all the various loan cost figures; the only thing missing is the totals.

What You Do	How You Do It
1. **Enter the totals for the three yearly columns and for the Principal row in the Loan Rates document.**	a. **Open Loan Rates.**
	b. **Choose View→Toolbars→Tables And Borders to display the Tables And Borders toolbar.**
	c. **In the table, place the insertion point in the empty cell at the bottom of the First Year column.**
	d. **On the Tables And Borders toolbar, click the AutoSum button** Σ **. The total ($3,008.29) appears in the cell.**
	e. **Place the insertion point in the empty cell at the bottom of the Second Year column.**
	f. **Click the AutoSum button.**
	g. **Place the insertion point in the empty cell at the bottom of the Third Year column.**
	h. **Click the AutoSum button.**
	i. **Place the insertion point in the first empty cell in the Total column, at the end of the Principal row.**
	j. **Click the AutoSum button.**
	k. **Close the Tables And Borders toolbar.**

2. Can you use AutoSum for the totals for the remaining rows? Why or why not?

---

3. **Enter the totals for the Interest and Annual Totals rows and save the document as *My Loan Rates*.**

   a. The numbers in the Interest row are all less than $1,000. No commas appear in these numbers, so you will have to tell Word to include the comma in the formula result. **Place the insertion point in the empty cell at the end of the Interest row.**

   b. **Choose Table→Formula.**

   c. The formula in the Formula text box defaults to =SUM(ABOVE). **Modify the formula to read =SUM(LEFT).**

   d. To include a comma and dollar signs in the formula result, from the Number Format drop-down list, **select the third number format.**

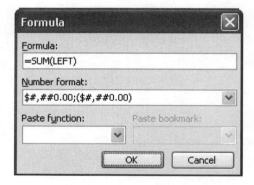

   e. **Click OK.**

   f. **Place the insertion point in the empty cell at the end of the Annual Totals row.**

   g. **Press F4** to repeat the calculation. This is the grand total of the cost over the life of the loan.

   h. **Save the document as *My Loan Rates***

TOPIC G

Create a Chart from a Word Table

In Topic 2F, you began to work with tables that contained numeric information. Another way to display numeric table information is to transform the table to a chart. In this topic, you'll create a chart from a Word table.

A picture is worth a thousand words and a chart is worth a tableful of numbers. If you want people to really respond to the numbers you're presenting in your table, and to really understand the relationships between the figures, don't just show them the table; show them a chart.

Charts

Definition:

A *chart,* also commonly referred to as a *graph,* is a visual representation of the relationships between one or more series of numbers. Charts can be a variety of types, such as column charts, line graphs, or pie charts. Charts can have any or all of the components listed in Table 2-4.

Table 2-4: *Chart Components*

Chart Component	Description
Category axis (X-axis); Value axis (Y-axis)	The axes are the lines showing values against which the chart data is plotted. Depending on the chart type, the X-axis can appear along the bottom or up the left side of the chart; the Y-axis is plotted at 90 degrees to the X-axis.
Scale	The range of values on the value axis. Derived from the values in the original table.
Axis labels	Descriptions of the data plotted against the category axis. Derived from text in the original table.
Legend	A visual indicator of which sections of the chart relate to which sets of values in the table. Derived from text in the original table.
Titles	Descriptive text added to the axes or the chart as a whole.
Data labels	Descriptive text added to individual values in the chart.

Example: A Column Chart

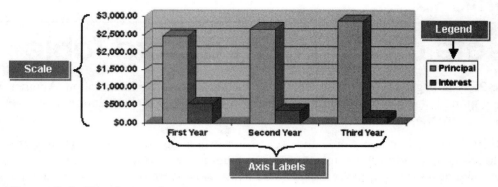

Figure 2-3: *A column chart.*

Microsoft Graph

Microsoft Graph is a supplemental application that provides the charting functions to Word and the other Microsoft Office applications. Whenever you create or modify a chart, Word automatically activates the Microsoft Graph functions and adds a Chart menu to the Word menu bar, and a Microsoft Graph Help entry to the Word Help menu.

How to Create a Chart from a Word Table

Procedure Reference: Create a Chart from a Word Table

To create a chart from a Word table:

1. Select the portion of the table that you wish to chart.

2. Choose Insert→Picture→Chart. The chart and associated datasheet appear in Microsoft Graph.

3. Double-click the letter or number headings of any columns or rows on the datasheet that you want to exclude from the chart.

4. Click the document to close Microsoft Graph and return to Word. The chart will be inserted immediately below the associated table.

5. Drag the sizing handles to change the size of the chart as needed.

6. Drag the chart or use Cut and Paste to move the chart as needed.

> If you do not have any table data selected when you choose Insert→Picture→Chart, Word will insert a chart with a generic datasheet at the insertion point.

The Table/Chart Relationship

Chart data is based on the chart's datasheet, not on the data in the table itself. Once you have created a chart from a table, there is no longer any relationship between the numbers in the table and the numbers in the chart's datasheet. Therefore, the chart will not automatically update if numbers in the table change.

ACTIVITY 2-7

Creating a Chart

Setup:

My Loan Rates is open.

Scenario:

To help your customers visualize and compare the principal and interest costs of their loans, you decide to create a chart of that information from the table data in your loan document. Once you create the chart, you realize that the default size and position of the chart are not in balance with the rest of the document.

What You Do	How You Do It
1. In My Loan Rates, **create the chart from the table data.**	a. **Select the table.**
	b. **Choose Insert→Picture→Chart** to display the chart and its associated datasheet.
	c. In the datasheet, **double-click the Row 3 row heading** to exclude the total row from the chart.
	d. In the datasheet, **double-click the Column D column heading** to exclude the total column from the chart.

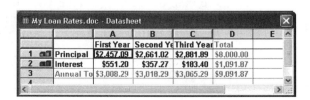

	e. **Click the document** to close the datasheet and verify the appearance of the chart.
2. **Size the chart proportionally with the size of the table.**	a. **Click the chart once** to select it and display the sizing handles.
	b. **Drag the bottom-right sizing handle down and to the right** to approximately **5 on the horizontal ruler and 6 on the vertical ruler** to increase the size of the chart.

3. Move the chart to the end of the document.

a. With the chart still selected, **choose Edit→Cut.**

> You can use the Cut and Paste toolbar buttons if you prefer.

b. **Place the insertion point on the last paragraph mark in the document.**

c. **Choose Edit→Paste** to move the chart and create some space between the chart and the table.

d. **Save the document.**

TOPIC H

Modify a Chart

In Topic 2G, you created a basic chart from a Word table. Once you create the chart, you can alter some of the chart's features and formatting. In this topic, you'll modify a chart.

You know how easy it is to create a complete basic chart from a Word table. But sometimes you need more than the basics. Maybe you need a pie chart, not a bar chart. Maybe you need to add some descriptive text. Maybe you need a 3D effect for maximum impact. You can modify the chart after it's created to fine-tune the chart's appearance.

Chart Types

There are several categories of chart types available in Microsoft Graph. Each type is designed to suit a particular type of data or to show a particular type of relationship. Some types have very similar uses; some types have extremely specialized applications. Within each category, there are sub-types that vary mainly in appearance.

Chart Types

Table 2-5 summarizes the main categories of chart types according to the type of data each chart type normally represents.

Table 2-5: *Chart Types*

Chart Type	Shows
Column, Bar, Cylinder, Cone, or Pyramid	Comparisons among categories of items. A bar chart is a column chart with the x-axis on the left instead of at the bottom of the chart. A cylinder, cone, or pyramid chart is like a column chart with columns in that particular shape.
Stacked Column, Stacked Bar, and other stacked chart types	Relations of parts to a whole.
Line or Area	Trends over time. An area chart is a line chart with the area under the line filled in.
Pie or Doughnut	Relations of parts to a whole. A pie chart shows a single set of numbers in a circle; a doughnut can show multiple data sets in concentric rings.
XY (Scatter)	Relations between pairs of values.
Bubble	Relations among three variables. Essentially it is an XYZ-type scatter chart; the size of the bubble represents the value of the third variable.
Radar	Comparisons between aggregate values in multiple sets of numbers.
Surface	Trends resulting from the combinations of two sets of data. Used to find the optimum combination of values for two variables.
Stock	High-low-close-open values for commodities traded in a market or exchange.

How to Modify a Chart

You can use Microsoft Graph to make various modifications to the chart. Two simple and common modifications are to change the chart type and to add title or axis labels to the chart.

Procedure Reference: Change the Chart Type

To change the chart type:

1. Double-click the chart to access the Microsoft Graph functions.

   If you want to see the datasheet associated with the chart, and the datasheet does not appear, choose View→Datasheet after you double-click the chart.

2. Choose Chart→Chart Type.

3. In the Chart Type list, select a category.

4. In the Chart Sub-Type area, select the specific chart type.

5. Click OK.

6. Click the document to close Microsoft Graph.

Procedure Reference: Add Title or Axis Labels

To add title or axis labels:

1. Double-click the chart to launch Microsoft Graph.

2. Choose Chart→Chart Options.

3. On the Titles tab, in the Chart Title text box, enter the chart title.

4. Enter the axis labels in the appropriate axis text boxes.

5. Click OK.

6. Click the document to close Microsoft Graph.

ACTIVITY 2-8

Modifying a Chart

Setup:

My Loan Rates is open.

Scenario:

After looking at your chart, you realize that it does not effectively represent the overall loan costs over time. It is also missing a descriptive title.

What You Do	How You Do It
1. In My Loan Rates, **change the chart type.**	a. You need to open the chart and its associated datasheet for editing. **Double-click the chart.**
	b. **Click the Close box for the datasheet** to close the datasheet.
	c. **Choose Chart→Chart Type.**
	d. A stacked column chart will show the total values over time. In the Chart Sub-Type box, **select the middle option in the second row.**

Chart sub-type:

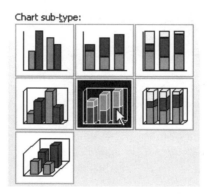

	e. **Click OK.**
2. **Add the chart title.**	a. **Choose Chart→Chart Options.**
	b. In the Chart Title text box, **type *Home Improvement Loan Costs***
	c. **Click OK.**
	d. **Click the document** to return to Word and verify the appearance of the chart.
	e. **Save and close the document.**

Lesson 2 Follow-up

In this lesson, you customized tables and charts. Customizing a table enables you to arrange, structure, and format your table to display table information in the most effective way. Plus, you can use the charting features of Word to display table information graphically to enhance the impact of the figures in your tables.

1. **What kind of tables and charts have you seen in the business documents that you work with?**

2. **Which of Word's table-customization features do you think you will find useful?**

LESSON 3
Customizing Formatting

Lesson Time
25 minutes

Lesson Objectives:

In this lesson, you will customize formatting.

You will:

- Modify character spacing.
- Add text effects.
- Control paragraph flow.

Introduction

You know from the previous course how to perform all the basic formatting of characters and paragraphs. As you produce more advanced documents, you might see the need for some specialized formatting. In this lesson, you will customize character and paragraph formatting.

Basic techniques of character and paragraph formatting will meet your needs in most cases. As you become a more advanced word-processing user, you'll encounter types of information that need something extra. Custom formatting options will give your documents the "just right" appearance that basic formats don't provide.

TOPIC A

Modify Character Spacing

In this lesson, you will apply specialized formatting to characters and paragraphs. One of the special character formats you can control is character spacing. In this topic, you will modify character spacing.

Character spacing is a very specialized formatting technique that can help you fine-tune the appearance of text in very specific instances. Character spacing is a great way to create a special look for text in a title or header, without having to introduce a new or different font into a document. Character spacing gives you the most precise control possible over text appearance.

Character Spacing Options

Character spacing options control the relative size of characters as well as the distance between, above, and below characters. You can set various options for character spacing.

Character Spacing Option	Effect
Scale	Increases or decreases character size proportionately by a given percentage.
Spacing	Expands or condenses all the characters evenly by a given number of *points*.
Position	Raises or lowers the text in relation to the baseline by a given number of points. Differs from superscript or subscript because it does not change the font size.
Kerning	Expands or condenses individual pairs of letters to create the appearance of even spacing. The effects of kerning are visible only in fairly large fonts, so kerning is applied only to characters above a given number of points.

How to Modify Character Spacing

Procedure Reference: Modify Character Spacing

To modify character spacing:

1. Select the text you want to format.

2. Open the Font dialog box:
   - Choose Format→Font, or
   - Right-click the selected text and choose Font.

3. Select the Character Spacing tab.

4. Select the character spacing options you need. You can see the results of your selections in the Preview box.

5. Click OK.

ACTIVITY 3-1

Modifying Character Spacing

Data Files:

- Burke Flyer.doc

Scenario:

You're preparing an advertising flyer and you would like to call more attention to the title of the document. However, you don't want to introduce an entirely new font style, as too many fonts will make the document look too busy. You can't simply make the title bigger, because your corporate style guidelines set a limit of 20 points for font titles. You also want to find a way to accentuate the portion of the document that refers to market ups and downs.

What You Do	How You Do It
1. Expand the character spacing for the title of the Burke Flyer document to 2 points.	a. Open Burke Flyer.
	b. In the first line of the document, **select the text "Burke Properties, Inc."**
	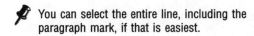 You can select the entire line, including the paragraph mark, if that is easiest.
	c. **Choose Format→Font.**
	d. **Select the Character Spacing tab.**
	e. From the Spacing drop-down list, **select Expanded.**
	f. In the first By text box, **enter *2 pt***

	g. **Click OK** to apply your custom character spacing to the title.
2. Set the character position for the "ups and downs" text.	a. In the second line of the first paragraph, **double-click the word "ups" to select it.**

· **About·Burke·Properties,·Inc.¶**
Because·Burke·Properties·is·a·full-service·real·¬
all·the·**ups**·and·downs·of·the·real·estate·market!

	b. **Choose Format→Font.**
	c. On the Character Spacing tab, from the Position drop-down list, **select Raised.**

	d. **Click OK** to raise the text by the default of 3 points.
	e. **Select the word "downs."**

f. Change the character spacing to lower the word "downs" by the default amount.

About·Burke·Properties,·Inc.¶
Because·Burke·Properties·is·a·full-service·real·
all·the·ᵘᵖˢ·and·₍downs₎·of·the·real·estate·market!

3. Save the document as *My Burke Flyer* and close the document.

a. Save the document as *My Burke Flyer*

b. Close the document.

TOPIC B

Add Text Effects

In Topic 3A, you modified character spacing, which is one example of an advanced character format. The other type of advanced character formatting you can use is text effects. In this topic, you will add text effects.

Text effects are a unique way to enhance your electronic documents. A well-chosen text effect can add interest to documents that your readers access electronically, such as an electronic newsletter, or an announcement you send attached to an email. Text effects give you a simple way to catch readers' attention, add sparkle, and enhance the visual interest of documents like these.

Text Effects

Text effects add motion and animation to selected text. For example, you can apply a text effect that adds a blinking background to a selected section of text. Text effects are visible only in the electronic version of the document; they do not appear in print.

How to Add Text Effects

Procedure Reference: Add Text Effects

To add text effects:

1. Select the text you want to format.

2. Open the Font dialog box:
    - Choose Format→Font, or
    - Right-click the selected text and choose Font.

3. Select the Text Effects tab.

4. Select the text effect you need from the Animations list. To remove a text effect, select None. You can see the results of your selections in the Preview box.

5. Click OK.

ACTIVITY 3-2

Adding Text Effects

Data Files:

- Company Picnic. doc

Scenario:

You're preparing an announcement of the Burke Properties company picnic. You've arranged with the Burke Properties Web master to post the announcement on the company's internal network. You want to promote this fun event, so you want to find a way to catch employees' attention when they open the document from the Web site.

What You Do	How You Do It
1. **Add a text effect to the title of the Company Picnic document.**	a. **Open Company Picnic.**
	b. **Select the first line of the document.**
	c. **Choose Format→Font.**
	d. **Select the Text Effects tab.**
	e. From the Animations list, **select Sparkle Text.**
	f. **Click OK.**
	g. To view the effect in the document, **click the next line** to deselect the title paragraph.
2. **Save the document as *My Company Picnic* and close the document.**	a. **Save the document as *My Company Picnic***
	b. **Close the document.**

TOPIC C

Control Paragraph Flow

This lesson covers advanced formatting options for both characters and paragraphs. So far, you've modified character formatting. You can also customize paragraph formatting by setting paragraph flow options. In this topic, you will control paragraph flow.

You've completed your document and most of it looks great. Time for one more proofread. Whoops! The larger fonts you've chosen for section titles mean that some of the paragraphs have wrapped a single line onto the top of the next page. There's a section heading on a different page from the first paragraph of the section. And it looks as if that chart you added towards the end has pushed one paragraph all by itself to the last page. It looks a little messy, and it's hard to read this way. But don't worry—it's easy to fix these little layout problems by setting options to control the paragraph flow.

Paragraph Flow Options

You can set several options to control paragraph flow.

Paragraph Flow Option	Effect
Widow/Orphan Control	Prevents *widows* (a single line at the top of a page) and *orphans* (a single line at the bottom of a page). Widow/Orphan Control is on by default.
Keep Lines Together	Prevents selected lines from splitting across a break.
Keep With Next	Ensures that the current paragraph will always appear on the same page as the paragraph that follows it. Useful for a heading or title paragraph that leads into a paragraph of text.
Page Break Before	Ensures that the paragraph will always be first on a page.

How to Control Paragraph Flow

Procedure Reference: Control Paragraph Flow

To control paragraph flow:

1. Place the insertion point inside a single paragraph, or select the multiple paragraphs.

2. Open the Paragraph dialog box:
   - Choose Format→Paragraph, or
   - Right-click the selection and choose Paragraph.

3. Select the Line And Page Breaks tab.

4. Select the options you need. You can see the results of your settings in the Preview box.

5. Click OK.

Activity 3-3

Controlling Paragraph Flow

Data Files:

- Stockholder Review.doc

Scenario:

You're preparing some text to include with the Burke Properties Annual Report. After drafting the text and inserting the graphics, you proofread the document to catch any problems with the formatting and layout. You notice that the figures in the document are printing on different pages from the paragraphs that introduce the figures.

What You Do	How You Do It
1. In Stockholder Review, **set the paragraph flow options so that the introductory paragraph stays with Figure 1.**	a. **Open Stockholder Review.**
	b. **Scroll to the bottom of the first page.**
	c. The last paragraph on the page begins "Figure 1 shows..." but the figure does not appear on the page. With the insertion point inside the "Figure 1 shows" paragraph, **choose Format→Paragraph.**
	d. **Select the Line And Page Breaks tab.**
	e. In the Pagination area, **verify that Widow/Orphan Control is checked. Check Keep With Next.**

Pagination

☑ Widow/Orphan control   ☑ Keep with next

☐ Keep lines together   ☐ Page break before

| | f. **Click OK** to move the paragraph to page 2, along with the figure. |

2. Set the paragraph flow options so that the introductory paragraph stays with Figure 2.

a. Scroll to find the reference to Figure 2.

b. The last paragraph on this page begins "Figure 2 shows...." but the figure does not appear on the page. With the insertion point inside the "Figure 2 shows" paragraph, **choose Format→Paragraph.**

c. On the Line And Page Breaks tab, **verify that Widow/Orphan Control is checked. Check Keep With Next.**

d. **Click OK** to move the paragraph to page 4, along with the figure.

You could also use the Repeat key (F4) to repeat the formatting.

3. Save the document as *My Stockholder Review* and close the document.

a. Save the document as *My Stockholder Review*

b. **Close the document.**

Lesson 3 Follow-up

In this lesson, you applied a variety of custom character and paragraph formats. These are a group of formatting techniques that you might not need every day, but which provide you options that can be useful when you encounter special situations that call for more variety or more precise control over the text appearance in a document.

1. **What documents have you seen that contain any of the custom formatting options discussed in this lesson?**

2. **Where do you think you might use custom formatting options in your own documents?**

NOTES

LESSON 4
Working with Custom Styles

Lesson Time
40 minutes

Lesson Objectives:

In this lesson, you will work with custom styles.

You will:

- Create a character or paragraph style.
- Modify an existing style.
- Create a list style.
- Create a table style.

Introduction

In the previous course and in Lesson 3, you learned how to apply all different types of formatting to characters and paragraphs. If you often use certain combinations of formatting options together, you can combine them in a custom style. In this lesson, you will work with custom styles.

Your business probably has a communications standard that defines a unique look for your documents. It might take some time to produce custom documents if you apply each format by hand. If you find yourself applying the same custom formatting over and over in different documents, then creating your own styles can make your life easier. Custom styles will give your documents the consistent, customized formatting you need with just a few clicks of the mouse.

TOPIC A

Create a Character or Paragraph Style

This lesson covers creating several different types of custom styles. The most basic styles include the most basic types of formatting: character and paragraph. In this topic, you will create character or paragraph styles.

You've become a formatting expert. You're familiar with all the different options that you have for character and paragraph formatting, and you're starting to develop a unique look for your documents by creating your own custom combinations of formats. For example, you love the Verdana, 14 pt, Bold Italic, Expanded combination for section headings. You wish it was easy to apply that combination of formats all the time. Well, you can; by creating your own custom style.

Common Style Types

The two most common types of styles are paragraph styles and character styles.

- Paragraph styles are the most common style type. They contain paragraph formatting, such as left, center, or right alignment, as well as character formatting, such as font size or type. Use paragraph styles when you are formatting an entire paragraph.

- Character styles contain only character formatting. Use character styles when you format sections of text within a paragraph.

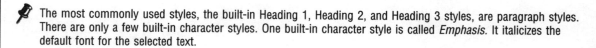

The most commonly used styles, the built-in Heading 1, Heading 2, and Heading 3 styles, are paragraph styles. There are only a few built-in character styles. One built-in character style is called *Emphasis*. It italicizes the default font for the selected text.

Microsoft® Word 2003: Level 2

Templates

Definition:

A *template* is a document that is used as a basis for creating other new documents. Word templates have the .dot file extension. Templates provide the basic structure, layout, and formatting of a document. Templates can store a variety of document elements, such as AutoText entries, the default document font, and page layout settings.

Example: The Normal Template

By default, every new Word document you create is based on the Normal template (Normal.dot). The Normal template also stores various default settings for the Word program.

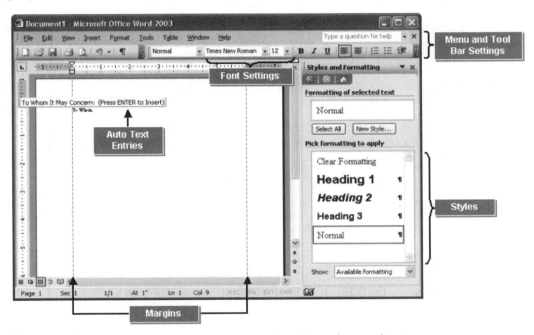

Figure 4-1: *A new document based on the Normal template.*

Template Types

There are two main categories of templates:

- *Document templates* are templates used to create specific kinds of documents. For example, Word provides templates to create various types of standard business documents such as letters and memos.

- *Global templates* are templates whose settings are available to all open Word documents. The Normal template is the only default global template. However, it is possible to load other document templates as global templates.

> See the Help system in Word for more information about templates.

How to Create a Character or Paragraph Style

Procedure Reference: Create a Custom Style

To create a custom style:

1. If you have example text that is formatted with properties similar to the ones you want to include in the style, select the example text.

2. Choose Format→Styles And Formatting to display the Styles And Formatting task pane.

3. Click New Style to open the New Style dialog box.

4. In the Name text box, enter a unique new name for the style.

5. From the Style Type drop-down list, select Character or Paragraph.

6. From the Style Based On drop-down list, select any existing character format (for new character styles) or paragraph style (for new paragraph styles) that you want to base this style on.

7. For a paragraph style, from the Style For Following Paragraph drop-down list, select a style, if you want a particular paragraph style always to follow this style.

8. Adjust any basic formatting settings in the Formatting area. The choices will vary depending upon whether you are creating a character or paragraph style.

9. If necessary, select additional formatting options:

   a. Click Format and select the category of formatting you need (Font, Paragraph, and so on).

   b. Set the options for each category and click OK.

10. Check Add To Template if you want the style to be available in other new documents based on the current template.

11. Click OK in the New Style dialog box to create the new style.

12. Test the style by applying it to any desired text.

Automatically Updating a Paragraph Style

Check Automatically Update in the New Style dialog box if you want to modify a paragraph style automatically any time you reformat text that uses the style .

Procedure Reference: Delete a Style

You can delete a custom style that you no longer need from a document. You cannot delete built-in styles.

To delete a custom style:

1. Display the Styles And Formatting task pane.

2. Click the style name in the list.

3. Click the arrow next to the style name and select Delete.

4. Click Yes to confirm the deletion. Text formatted with the style will revert either to the Normal style, or to whatever other style was originally applied to the selection.

🖋 You can also use the Organizer to delete styles from documents or templates. See the Microsoft Office Word Help system for more information.

Using Custom Styles in Other Documents

To use a new custom style in other existing documents, copy some text that is formatted with the style to the other documents and save the documents. You can then delete the copied text from the target document. The style will be saved with the document.

ACTIVITY 4-1

Creating a Custom Style

Data Files:

- Formatted Flyer.doc

- About Us.doc

Scenario:

You're working on two separate marketing pieces and you want to set off the text Burke Properties wherever it appears in each document. In one of the documents, you've formatted the first item the way you want it, but you're afraid it is going to take a long time to apply it by hand everywhere else in both documents.

What You Do	How You Do It
1. Create a custom style based on the specially formatted Burke Properties text in the Formatted Flyer document.	a. **Open Formatted Flyer.** b. The words "Burke Properties" appear with special formatting in the first line of the first full paragraph. In the first line of the first full paragraph, **select the text "Burke Properties"**

·About·Our·Firm¶

Founded·in·1946·by·John·Burke,·▐BURKE PROPERTIES·is·

c. **Choose Format→Styles And Formatting** to display the Styles And Formatting task pane.

d. **Click New Style.**

e. In the Name text box, **type *BP Name*** as the style name.

f. From the Style Type drop-down list, **select Character.**

g. **Verify that the style will be based on the default paragraph font with the additional formatting.**

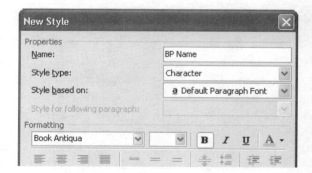

h. **Click OK** to create the style.

2. **Apply the new style to the other Burke Properties text and save the document as *My Formatted Flyer*.**

a. In the second line of the first full paragraph, **select the text Burke Properties.**

b. In the Pick Formatting To Apply list in the Styles And Formatting task pane, **click BP Name.**

c. In the first line of the second full paragraph, **select the text Burke Properties.**

d. In the Styles And Formatting task pane, **click BP Name.**

e. **Save the document as *My Formatted Flyer***

3. **Copy the text with the new style into the first section of the About Us document.**

a. In My Formatted Flyer, **verify that the Burke Properties text is still selected and choose Edit→Copy.**

b. **Open About Us.**

c. At the beginning of the first full paragraph, under the About Us heading, **select the text Burke Properties.**

    About·Us¶
    Burke·Properties·is·a·full-service·

d. **Choose Edit→Paste.**

e. **Choose Format→Styles And Formatting.** The BP Name style appears in the Pick Formatting To Apply list.

4. **Apply the custom style to the Burke Properties text in the other sections of About Us.**

a. Under the Description of Our Firm subheading, **select the Burke Properties text.**

b. **Click BP Name to apply the style.**

c. Under the Our Goal subheading, **apply the style to the Burke Properties text.**

5. Save the document as *My About Us* and close the document.

   a. Save the document as *My About Us*

   b. Close the document.

Topic B

Modify an Existing Style

In Topic 4A, you created new custom styles. Another way to create a customized style is to modify a style that already exists. In this topic, you'll modify an existing style.

There are two great benefits to modifying an existing style rather than building your own from scratch. One is that there might be a style that is close to what you want for your custom style. You can save time by using the existing style as a starting point for your customization. Plus, modifying a style you've already applied to a document is a quick way to change the formatting consistently throughout that document. If you know how to modify styles, you'll have a quick way to update the formatting in your documents.

How to Modify an Existing Style

Procedure Reference: Modify a Style Using Example Text

The easiest way to modify a style is to base it on example text. To modify a style using example text:

1. Modify the example text to include the properties you want in your style.

2. Select the example text.

3. Display the Styles And Formatting task pane.

4. In the Styles And Formatting task pane, click the arrow next to the name of the style you want to modify.

5. Choose Update To Match Selection to modify the style and apply your changes to any text in the current document that uses the style.

Procedure Reference: Modify a Style Manually

You can also modify a style manually by using the Modify Style dialog box. To modify a style manually:

1. In the Styles And Formatting task pane, click the arrow next to the name of the style you want to modify.

2. Choose Modify.

3. Select the options you want in the Modify Style dialog box. You have the same choices and options you would have if you were creating a new style, including the option to add the style to the template.

4. Click OK to save your changes and apply them to any text that uses the style.

Modifying a Style in Other Documents

If you modify a style in a document, the modifications are applied to all text formatted with that style in the current document. However, it does not update text in other documents that is formatted with the style. One way to update the style in another document is to delete the style in the other document. Then, copy some text formatted with the modified style to the other document just as you would with a new style.

ACTIVITY 4-2

Modifying a Style

Setup:

My Formatted Flyer is open.

Scenario:

You've decided that the Burke Properties text in your flyer would look even more impressive if it had the Burke Properties pale blue coloring. It would save time if you could update all instances of the text at the same time.

What You Do	How You Do It
1. **Add pale blue color to the format of the first Burke Properties text in My Formatted Flyer.**	a. In My Formatted Flyer, **select the Burke Properties text in the paragraph that begins with, "Founded in 1946..."**
	b. **Choose Format→Font.**
	c. **Select the Font tab.**
	d. On the Font tab of the dialog box, **click the Font Color drop-down list arrow** to open the Font Color drop-down list.
	e. **Select the Pale Blue color in the bottom row.**

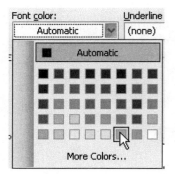

f. **Click OK** to apply the color to the selected text.

2. Modify the custom BP Name style to match the new formatting and close My Formatted Flyer.

a. Verify that the text is still selected.

b. In the Styles And Formatting task pane, click the down arrow next to the BP Name style.

c. Choose Update To Match Selection.

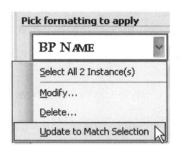

Pick formatting to apply

BP NAME

Select All 2 Instance(s)

Modify...

Delete...

Update to Match Selection

d. The new format is applied to all sections of text that have the BP Name style applied. **Save and close My Formatted Flyer.**

e. **Close the Styles And Formatting task pane.**

TOPIC C

Create a List Style

In the first topics in this lesson, you worked with character and paragraph styles. In the remaining topics in this lesson, you will create styles that contain formats for specific document components. In this topic, you'll create a list style.

Formatting a list involves setting formats for the characters, the paragraph, and for the custom list options such as bullet style and spacing. If you've put in the time it takes to modify all the settings to get just the right list appearance, you can preserve that combination in a list style. List styles give you a way to incorporate and apply all the formatting settings you want for your list items.

How to Create a List Style

Procedure Reference: Create a Custom List Style

To create a custom list style:

1. Select example list text that is formatted with properties similar to the ones you want to include in the style, if you have any such example text.

2. Apply any additional formatting to the example list text. You can also apply formatting later, as you create the style.

3. Choose Format→Styles And Formatting to display the Styles And Formatting task pane.

4. Click New Style to open the New Style dialog box.

5. In the Name text box, enter a unique new name for the style.

6. From the Style Type drop-down list, select List.

7. Adjust any basic formatting settings in the Formatting area.

8. If necessary, select additional formatting options:

    a. Click Format and select the category of formatting you need.

    b. Set the options for each category and click OK.

9. Check Add To Template if you want the style to be available in other new documents.

10. Click OK in the New Style dialog box to create the new style.

11. Test the style by applying it to any desired list.

ACTIVITY 4-3

Creating a List Style

Data Files:

*   List Style.doc

Scenario:

As the human resources manager for Burke Properties, you find that you often create lists of instructions that have a similar format—a numbered list with a second level of bulleted items. You have been customizing each of your lists by hand to achieve this appearance, but this is very time consuming.

What You Do	How You Do It
1. **Create the BP List style based on the list in the List Style document. Save the document as _My List Style_.**	a. **Open List Style.**
	b. This document contains a list with customized formatting. In the body of the memo, **drag to select the list text from item 1 through the last bulleted item.**
	c. **Choose Format→Styles And Formatting** to open the Styles And Formatting task pane.
	d. **Click New Style.**
	e. In the Name text box, **type _BP List_**
	f. From the Style Type drop-down list, **select List.**
	g. **Check Add To Template.**
	h. **Click OK** to create the style.
	i. **Save the document as _My List Style_**
	j. **Close the document.**

2. **Test the list style.**

a. On the Standard toolbar, **click the New Blank Document button** .

b. In the Styles And Formatting task pane, in the Pick Formatting To Apply list, **select BP List.**

c. The number style for the first level of the list has been applied to the blank paragraph. **Type** *first line test* **and press Enter** to move to a new line.

d. To demote this paragraph and apply the bullet style for the second list level, **press Tab.**

e. **Close the new document without saving changes.**

f. **Close the Styles And Formatting task pane.**

TOPIC D

Create a Table Style

You've now created character, paragraph, and list styles. The last type of style you can create in Word is a table style. In this topic, you'll create a table style.

Like list styles, table styles incorporate not only basic formatting settings such as your font choice, but also table-specific settings such as the borders, shading, and text alignment. It would be tedious to have to re-create all those settings by hand if you want to start a new table with the same look. If you have a great-looking table and you want to reproduce that look consistently and quickly in other tables, then a table style is a great tool for you.

How to Create a Table Style

Procedure Reference: Create a Custom Table Style

Unlike the other style types, you cannot create a table style from an example table. You must create it by selecting the table formatting options in the New Style dialog box.

To create a custom table style:

1. Open the New Style dialog box: Choose Format→Styles And Formatting to display the Styles And Formatting task pane.

   • Click New Style in the Styles And Formatting task pane, or

- Choose Table→Table AutoFormat and click New.

2. In the Name text box, enter a unique new name for the style.

3. From the Style Type drop-down list, select Table.

4. From the Style Based On drop-down list, select any existing table style that you want to base this style on. The default is Table Normal.

5. From the Apply Formatting To drop-down list, select the portion of the table you want to apply the style to.

6. Adjust any basic formatting settings in the Formatting area.

7. If necessary, select additional formatting options:

   a. Click Format and select the category of formatting you need.

   b. Set the options for each category and click OK.

8. Check Add To Template if you want the style to be available in other new documents.

9. Click OK in the New Style dialog box to create the new style.

10. Click OK to close the Table AutoFormat dialog box (if it is open).

11. Test the style by applying it to any desired table.

    - Create a table, select it, and apply the style from the Styles And Formatting task pane, or

    - Choose Table→Insert→Table, click AutoFormat, select the style from the Table Styles list, and click OK twice.

Activity 4-4

Creating a Table Style

Scenario:

As an agent for Burke Properties, you find that you often create tables of information that have a similar format. You have been customizing each of your tables by hand to achieve this appearance, but this is taking too much time.

What You Do	How You Do It
1. In a blank document, **create a table style called BP Table based on the Table Normal style.**	a. **Open a new, blank document.**
	b. **Choose Table→Table AutoFormat.**
	c. **Click New** to open the New Style dialog box
	d. In the Name text box, **type *BP Table*.**
	e. **Verify that the new style will be based on the existing Table Normal style.** You can see the current formatting of the Table Normal style in the preview area.

2. **Format the header row to be bold, center aligned, and shaded pale blue.**

a. In the Apply Formatting To drop-down list, select Header Row.

b. **Click the Bold button.**

c. **Click the Alignment drop-down arrow and select Align Center.**

d. **Click the Fill Color drop-down list arrow and select Pale Blue.**

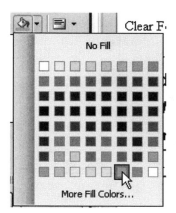

3. **Format the whole table to have the default borders.**

a. From the Apply Formatting To drop-down list, **select Whole Table.**

b. **Click the All Borders button** 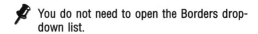 **.**

> You do not need to open the Borders drop-down list.

4. **Save the completed table style and save the document as** *My Table Style***.**

   a. **Verify the table appearance in the pre-view area and check Add To Template.**

   b. **Click OK to close the New Style dialog box.**

   c. **Click Close to close the Table AutoFormat dialog box.**

   d. **Save the document as** *My Table Style*

   e. **Close the document.**

5. **Test the table style in a new document.**

   a. **On the Standard toolbar, click the New Blank Document button .**

   b. **Choose Table→Insert→Table.**

   c. **Click AutoFormat.**

   d. **Scroll to the top of the styles list and select BP Table.**

   e. **Click OK.**

   f. **Click OK to create the table and apply the table style.**

   g. **Close the new document without saving changes.**

Lesson 4 Follow-up

In this lesson, you worked with custom styles. Custom styles enable you to create the custom formatting you need for your business documents and apply it quickly and consistently everywhere it is needed.

1. **Can you think of situations where you might need to combine several formats to create a custom look?**

2. **How would using a custom style make this kind of formatting easier for you?**

LESSON 5
Modifying Pictures

Lesson Time
25 minutes

Lesson Objectives:

In this lesson, you will modify pictures in a document.

You will:

- Set picture contrast or brightness.
- Crop a picture.
- Set text wrapping style for a picture.

Introduction

In the previous course, you learned how to insert pre-made graphics, including Clip Art items and pictures from files, into your documents. You can modify those pictures in various ways after they are inserted. In this lesson, you will modify pictures in your documents.

You don't have to be an artist to add great-looking graphics to your document. You can put an existing picture, such as a Word Clip Art element, into your document to add visual interest quickly and easily. But you don't have to stop there—you can also modify the default appearance of the pictures you insert to get a custom look.

TOPIC A

Set Picture Contrast or Brightness

This lesson covers various ways that you can modify pictures that you have inserted into your document. One of the most common modifications you can make to pictures is to adjust the contrast or brightness. In this topic, you will control picture contrast and brightness.

Being able to set a picture's contrast and brightness means that you have the ability to control just how prominent a picture is on the page. The statement your picture makes can be bold or subtle; it can be in the foreground or the background; it can grab attention or just lend atmosphere. The contrast and brightness settings are your main tools for achieving these effects.

Contrast and Brightness Settings

The *contrast* setting on a graphic element controls the amount of difference between adjacent colors or shades of gray in the image. Contrast is set as a percentage. A picture with zero contrast will be gray; a picture with 100 percent contrast will contain only black, white, and primary colors. The contrast setting does not affect the portions of the picture that are pure white.

The *brightness* setting on an image changes the amount of white present in the colors or shades of gray in the image. Brightness is set as a percentage. A picture with zero brightness will be black (except for those portions of the image that were pure white); a picture with 100 percent brightness will be white. The brightness setting does not affect the portions of the picture that are pure white.

How to Set Picture Contrast or Brightness

You can set contrast and brightness by using the Picture toolbar or by using the Format Picture dialog box.

Procedure Reference: Set Contrast and Brightness with the Format Picture Dialog Box

Use the Format Picture dialog box when you need to set exact values for contrast and brightness. To set contrast and brightness with the Format Picture dialog box:

1. Open the Format Picture dialog box:
    *   Select the picture and choose Format→Picture, or

- Double-click the picture.

The dialog box should open with the Picture tab selected.

2. On the Picture tab, set the brightness value:
   - Move the Brightness slider until the percentage value is set to the value you want, or
   - Select the Brightness value directly in the Brightness text box.

3. On the Picture tab, set the contrast value:
   - Move the Contrast slider until the percentage value is set to the value you want, or
   - Select the Contrast value directly in the Contrast text box.

4. Click OK.

Procedure Reference: Set Contrast or Brightness with the Picture Toolbar

Use the Picture toolbar when you want to judge the values for contrast and brightness based on the appearance of the picture. To set contrast or brightness with the Picture toolbar:

1. Select the picture. This will display the Picture toolbar.

2. Click the More Contrast, Less Contrast, More Brightness, or Less Brightness buttons until the picture has the appearance you want.

The Picture Toolbar

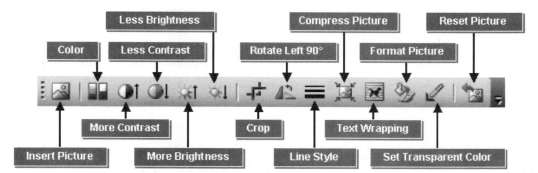

Figure 5-1: *The Picture toolbar.*

Resetting a Picture

If you need to experiment with different settings for picture appearance, you might occasionally need to return to the default settings for the picture. If so, you can reset the picture to its original appearance. On the Picture toolbar, click the Reset Picture button, or click Reset on the Picture tab of the Format Picture dialog box.

ACTIVITY 5-1

Setting Picture Contrast and Brightness

Data Files:

- Picture Flyer.doc

Scenario:

You're preparing a promotional flyer to help clients understand and appreciate the company's history and values. A picture will help set the right mood. However, once you insert the picture, you realize that its darkness and intensity will distract the reader's attention from the text.

What You Do	How You Do It
1. In the Picture Flyer document, **insert the Clip Art picture of a house on a lake at the beginning of the first text paragraph.**	a. **Open Picture Flyer.**
	b. **Place the insertion point at the beginning of the paragraph that begins "Founded in 1946...."**
	c. **Choose Insert→Picture→Clip Art** to open the Clip Art task pane.
	d. In the Search For text box, **type** *home* **and click Go.**
	e. The first picture shows a home reflected in a lake. **Click the first picture** to insert it into the document at the insertion point.

2. **Set the picture's brightness to 80% and its contrast to 20% and save the document as *My Picture Flyer*.**

a. In the document, **double-click the picture** to open the Format Picture dialog box.

b. Currently, both brightness and contrast are set to 50%. On the Picture tab, **select the current value in the Brightness text box.**

c. **Enter *80* as the new brightness value.**

d. **Change the Contrast value to 20.**

e. **Click OK** to apply the new brightness and contrast settings to the picture.

f. **Save the document as *My Picture Flyer***

TOPIC B

Crop a Picture

This lesson deals with several ways to modify pictures. Another common modification you might make is to change the picture's size or shape by cropping it. In this topic, you will crop a picture.

Cropping lets you take an existing picture and use just the parts of the picture you need. Do you have a square picture and a long, thin empty spot in your document? Do you love the boat in the picture but don't want to show the dock? Too much grass, not enough sky? No problem—just crop the picture to fit your requirements.

Cropping Options

Cropping a picture removes portions of the picture and also reduces the size of the picture. You can crop content as a straight line from the top, bottom, left, or right edges of the picture. The amount to crop is expressed as a value in inches or fractions of an inch. A negative cropping value adds white space to a given edge of the picture.

How to Crop a Picture

Procedure Reference: Crop a Picture with the Picture Toolbar

Use the Picture toolbar to crop a picture when you can set approximate values and you want to judge the cropping visually. To crop a picture with the Picture toolbar:

1. Display the Picture toolbar.

2. Click the Crop button. Cropping handles appear around the picture. The mouse pointer changes to a cropping tool shape.

3. Drag the cropping handles until the picture is cropped correctly.

4. Click the Crop button again to turn off the cropping handles and cropping tool.

Procedure Reference: Crop a Picture with the Format Picture Dialog Box

Use the Format Picture dialog box to crop precise amounts from the picture. To crop a picture with the Format Picture dialog box:

1. Double-click the picture to open the Format Picture dialog box and select the Picture tab.

2. In the Crop From area, set the values that you want in the Left, Right, Top, and Bottom text boxes.

3. Click OK.

Procedure Reference: Size or Scale a Picture Manually

After cropping a picture, you might need to readjust the size of the picture relative to your text. To resize or scale a picture manually:

1. Open the Format Picture dialog box and select the Size tab.

2. Enter sizing options if you want to set exact size values:
   - Enter a height value in the Height text box.
   - Enter a width value in the Width text box.

3. Enter scaling options if you want to adjust the size of the picture proportionately:
   - Check Lock Aspect Ratio if you want the height and width to scale proportionately to each other; uncheck it if you want the height and width to scale separately.
   - Check Relative To Original Picture Size if you want to scale the picture relative to its original size; uncheck it if you want to scale the picture relative to its current size.
   - Enter the scaling values for height, width, or both.

4. Click OK.

ACTIVITY 5-2

Cropping a Picture

Setup:

My Picture Flyer is open.

Scenario:

You want the picture in your document to focus on the beautiful home in the picture, rather than the landscape that surrounds it. However, you want to keep the picture at a size that balances the text in your document.

What You Do	How You Do It

1. In My Picture Flyer, **crop the picture to remove most of the landscape from the bottom and left side of the picture.**
 	
  If you crop more than you want, you can use Undo to restore the picture.
	a. On the Picture toolbar, **click the Crop button.**
	
	  The Picture toolbar should have opened when you opened the Format Picture dialog box in the previous activity. If it is not open, you can choose View→Toolbars→Picture to display it.
	
	 b. **Place the mouse pointer with the cropping tool over the center handle on the bottom border of the picture.**
	
	 c. **Drag the bottom border up to the bottom of the reflection of the house.**
	
	 d. **Use the cropping tool to drag the left border in closer to the house.**

	 Founded· a·full-service·real·estate·agency.·Not·only·do·ᵥ properties,·Burke·Properties·can·also·handle·y
	
	 e. On the Picture toolbar, **click the Crop button** to turn off the cropping tool.

2. **Scale the picture to increase its size to 150%.**

a. **Double-click the picture** to open the Format Picture dialog box.

b. **Select the Size tab.**

c. **Verify that Lock Aspect Ratio is checked.**

d. **With Lock Aspect Ratio checked, you can set the height value and automatically update the Width value. In the Scale area, in the Height text box, enter *150* to increase the height of the picture by 150%.**

e. **Press Tab to verify that the Width scaling value will be set to 150.**

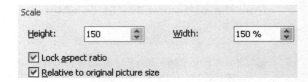

f. **Click OK to scale the picture.**

g. **Save the document.**

TOPIC C

Wrap Text Around a Picture

In the first topics of this lesson, you changed a picture's appearance and shape. Once the picture itself is formatted correctly, you can adjust the way the surrounding text fits with the picture. In this topic, you will wrap text around a picture.

Pictures in a document don't usually stand alone—most of a document is text, and the pictures have meaning in relationship to the text. If the text is too far away from the picture, obscured by the picture, or misaligned with the picture, you won't be getting your message across. Use text wrapping options to get the best visual effect from the pictures and text in your document.

Text Wrapping Styles

The text wrapping style on a graphic determines how the adjacent text will appear with the graphic. The text wrapping style determines whether the graphic is an *inline graphic,* which appears in the text at the insertion point, or a *floating graphic,* which is stored in a drawing layer separate from the text layer and can be positioned anywhere. You can configure floating graphics to align horizontally to the left, right, or center, or you can drag them to a specific location.

Text Wrapping Styles

There are five basic text wrapping styles.

Wrapping Style	Graphic Type	Text Wraps
In Line With Text	Inline	According to the shape and placement of the graphic.
Square	Floating	In a square shape around the graphic.
Tight	Floating	As close to the shape of the graphic as possible.
Behind Text	Floating	Across the front of the graphic.
In Front Of Text	Floating	Behind the graphic.

Advanced Wrapping Options

There are some advanced text wrapping options as well. For example, you can control the amount of white space between the graphic and the text wrapped around it. Or you can configure the text to wrap only on one side of the picture. See the Microsoft Office Word Help system for more information.

How to Set Text Wrapping Style for a Picture

Procedure Reference: Set Text Wrapping Style for a Picture

To set the text wrapping style for a picture.

1. Open the Format Picture dialog box.

2. Select the Layout tab.

3. Select the Wrapping Style option you prefer.

4. Select the Horizontal Alignment option you prefer. (This option is not available for the In Line With Text wrapping style.)

5. Click OK.

ACTIVITY 5-3

Setting the Text Wrapping Style for a Picture

Setup:

My Picture Flyer is open.

Scenario:

Now that your picture's size, shape, and appearance are set, you're ready to decide where to place the picture in your flyer.

What You Do	How You Do It
1. In My Picture Flyer, **set the text wrapping style for the picture so that it is set square with the text and to the right.**	a. **Double-click the picture** to open the Format Picture dialog box.
	b. **Select the Layout tab.**
	c. In the Wrapping Style section, **click Square.**
	d. In the Horizontal Alignment section, **select Right.**
	e. **Click OK.**
	f. The picture is now set to the right of the flyer text as desired. **Save and close the document.**
	g. **Close the Clip Art task pane.**

Lesson 5 Follow-up

In this lesson, you modified the appearance of pictures that you insert into your document. Whether you need to set the contrast and brightness to change the overall effect of a picture; crop the picture to fit your shape and size requirements; or set the text wrapping properties so your picture lines up properly with your text, modifying the picture enables you to customize the look of any picture in your document to suit your requirements for graphics.

1. **What are some of the effects that you have seen on graphics in the business documents that you work with?**

2. **How do you think you might use the picture-modification techniques presented in this lesson?**

LESSON 6

Creating Customized Graphic Elements

Lesson Time
35 minutes

Lesson Objectives:

In this lesson, you will create customized graphic elements.

You will:

*   Draw shapes and lines.
*   Insert WordArt.
*   Insert text boxes.
*   Create diagrams.

Introduction

In Lesson 5, you worked with pictures that you inserted from files or from Clip Art. You can also create your own graphic objects in your documents. In this lesson, you will create customized graphic elements.

Suppose that you need customized graphics in your document, but you can't find a Clip Art item or picture file that exactly fits. Relax—you don't have to be limited to what's available in the Clip Art Gallery. Whether you need to create an unusual look for your document titles; draw lines, arrows, or geometric shapes; or build personalized business diagrams, you can use Word to create your own custom graphic elements to add variety and complexity to your documents.

TOPIC A

Draw Shapes and Lines

This lesson covers adding many different types of custom graphic objects to your documents. The simplest types of objects you can add are geometric elements such as shapes and lines. In this topic, you will draw shapes and lines.

Creating your own shapes and lines is a practical way to add customized graphics to documents. Whether it's an arrow making a point, a splashy-looking header for a paragraph, or a banner for your document's title, Word's drawing tools make it easy to create shapes and lines accurately for the effect you want.

Drawing Object Options

You can control a variety of properties for drawn objects.

Drawing Object Option	Controls
AutoShapes	The basic style of the shape or line you insert. AutoShapes are divided into various categories including lines, arrows, and basic geometric shapes.
Fill Color	The color inside a shape.
Line Color	The color of a line or arrow or of the outside of a shape.
Font Color	The color of text added to a graphic object.
Line Style	The weight, thickness, and basic appearance of a line. For example, you can choose a double line or a single line.
Dash Style	Whether a line is dashed or dotted, and the pattern and appearance of the dashes or dots.
Arrow Style	The appearance and placement of arrowheads on an arrow object. For example, you can choose a double- or single-headed arrow.

Drawing Object Option	Controls
Shadow Style	If an object has a drop shadow behind it, and the general appearance of the shadow.
3-D Style	If an object has a 3-D effect, and the general 3-D appearance.
Grouping	If multiple objects can be treated as a unit for sizing, moving, or rotating.
Order	If an object appears in front or in back of other objects. Each floating object you draw is stacked on top of other objects in its own drawing layer. You can use the Order property to change the order of the layers in the stack.
Alignment	How floating objects are aligned in relation to other objects, to the drawing canvas, or to the page.
Distribution	The amount of horizontal or vertical space between multiple objects on a drawing canvas or on a page.

For more information on any of these options, see the Microsoft Office Word Help system.

The Drawing Toolbar

The Drawing toolbar contains several buttons and tools to help you work with graphic and drawn elements.

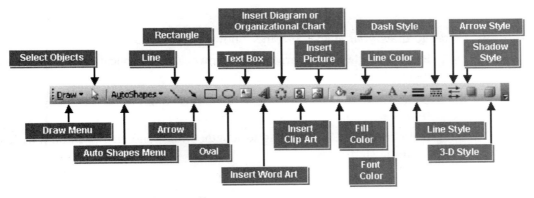

Figure 6-1: *The Drawing toolbar.*

The Drawing Canvas

The *drawing canvas* is a workspace for grouping, moving, and resizing drawn objects. By default, when you create a drawing, Word first inserts the drawing canvas inline with your text at the insertion point. You can then draw your shape within the canvas. The drawing canvas is most useful if you are creating a compound drawing consisting of several shapes, because it enables you to move and resize all the elements of the drawing as a unit.

 The drawing canvas is itself a drawn object, and you can resize and format it to create a decorative frame for your graphics.

Turning off the Drawing Canvas

If you prefer to work without the drawing canvas, you can configure Word not to insert it. Choose Tools→Options. On the General tab, uncheck Automatically Create Drawing Canvas When Inserting AutoShapes.

How to Draw Shapes and Lines

Procedure Reference: Draw Shapes and Lines

To draw shapes and lines in a document:

1. Place the insertion point where you want the graphic to appear.

2. Choose Insert→Picture→AutoShape. This will display the Drawing toolbar as well as the AutoShapes toolbar.

   > You can also display the Drawing toolbar by right-clicking the Standard toolbar and choosing Drawing, or choosing View→Toolbars→Drawing.

3. Select the AutoShape you want:
   - Select one of the default shapes on the Drawing toolbar, or
   - Click the AutoShapes button on the Drawing toolbar, select a category, and select a shape, or
   - Click a category on the AutoShapes toolbar and select a shape.

   Once you have selected a shape, the drawing canvas will appear in your document.

4. Press Esc to remove the drawing canvas if you prefer to draw outside the canvas.

5. Drag to draw your shape. Use the following guidelines:
   - For the single-headed arrow, the arrowhead will appear where you release the mouse button.
   - Hold down Shift as you drag to draw lines and arrows at 15-degree angles from the starting point.
   - Hold down Ctrl as you drag to lengthen lines and arrows in both directions from the starting point.
   - Hold down Shift as you drag to create proportionate shapes, such as drawing a circle with the Oval tool or a square with the Rectangle tool.

6. With the shape selected, set formatting options for the shape:
   - Choose Format→AutoShape and select the options you want on the Colors And Lines tab, or
   - Click the various formatting buttons on the Drawing toolbar (Fill Color, Line Color, Line Style, and so on) to set each option individually.

   > You can use the Format→AutoShape dialog box to set other picture properties for drawn graphics, such as Size and Layout.

7. Drag the sizing handles on the AutoShape to change the size and shape of the object as needed.

8. Drag the Rotate Point (the green dot) to turn the object as needed.

9. If you are using the drawing canvas, use the sizing handles on the corners of the drawing canvas to resize the canvas as needed.

10. Set other properties for the graphic as needed, such as the text wrapping style.

Procedure Reference: Remove an Object from the Drawing Canvas

To remove an object from the drawing canvas after you have drawn it:

1. Select the drawn object.

2. Drag the object outside the drawing canvas.

3. Click inside the drawing canvas.

4. With the insertion point inside the drawing canvas, press Delete to delete the drawing canvas.

5. Drag the object to the proper location in the document.

The Next Page and Previous Page Buttons

You can use the Next Page and Previous Page buttons below the vertical scroll bar to jump quickly from the top of one page to the top of another.

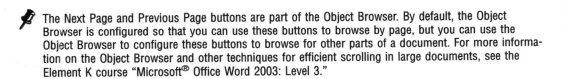

Figure 6-2: *The Next Page and Previous Page buttons.*

The Next Page and Previous Page buttons are part of the Object Browser. By default, the Object Browser is configured so that you can use these buttons to browse by page, but you can use the Object Browser to configure these buttons to browse for other parts of a document. For more information on the Object Browser and other techniques for efficient scrolling in large documents, see the Element K course "Microsoft® Office Word 2003: Level 3."

ACTIVITY 6-1

Drawing a Shape

Data Files:

* Burke Graphics.doc

Scenario:

You're working on a two-page promotional flyer for Burke Properties. You've entered all the text for the flyer, and what's missing now is the graphic elements. One area of the document you want to call attention to is the final paragraph, which contains the call to action for the customer.

What You Do	How You Do It
1. **Draw a star outside the drawing canvas at the beginning of the last paragraph of the Burke Graphics document.**	a. **Open Burke Graphics.**
	b. On the vertical scroll bar, **click the Next Page button** to move to the top of the second page of the document.
	c. The last paragraph of the document begins "You're the star at Burke Properties!" **Place the insertion point at the empty paragraph mark before the last paragraph of the document.**
	d. **Choose Insert→Picture→AutoShapes** to display the Drawing and AutoShapes toolbars.
	e. On the AutoShapes toolbar, **click the Stars And Banners button** [icon].
	f. **Click the 5-Point Star.**
	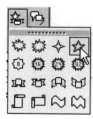
	g. When you select the AutoShape, the drawing canvas appears in the document. **Press Esc to remove the drawing canvas.**

h. When you begin drawing, the shape will appear on top of the adjacent text. **Drag to draw a small star approximately 1/2-inch high.**

i. **Close the AutoShapes toolbar.**

---

2. **Change the fill color of the graphic to pale blue.**

a. On the Drawing toolbar, **click the Fill Color arrow.**

b. **Click the Pale Blue fill color in the bottom row.**

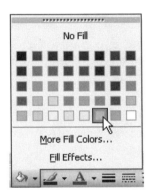

---

3. **Set the text wrapping properties for the object so that the star is in line with the text, and save the document as *My Burke Graphics.***

a. **Double-click the star** to open the Format AutoShape dialog box.

b. On the Layout tab, **select In Line With Text** as the wrapping style.

c. **Click OK.**

d. **Click in the last paragraph** to deselect and view the shape.

e. **Save the document as** *My Burke Graphics*

TOPIC B

Insert WordArt

In Topic 6A, you created generic graphic elements such as shapes and lines. You can also enhance the document with a type of graphic object that is unique to Word: WordArt. In this topic, you will insert WordArt.

Microsoft WordArt is a unique combination—part text, part graphics—so you can weave graphic interest directly in with your text. If you want an unusual look for small blocks of text such as titles or section headings, WordArt can be a great tool.

WordArt

WordArt is a Microsoft Office System tool that enables you to create decorative text elements as graphic objects in a document. WordArt provides you with a gallery of pre-defined WordArt effects, which include shapes, colors, and shading for the WordArt object. You provide the custom WordArt text. You can further customize WordArt by changing various WordArt font properties such as the font style, size, and alignment. You can also size or format WordArt as you would any other graphic object.

 There are various additional custom formatting options for WordArt available on the WordArt toolbar.

How to Insert WordArt

Procedure Reference: Insert WordArt

To insert WordArt:

1. Place the insertion point where you want the WordArt to appear.

    You can convert existing text to WordArt. Select the text before you display the WordArt gallery.

2. Display the WordArt gallery:
   * Choose Insert→Picture→WordArt, or

- Click the Insert WordArt button on the Drawing toolbar.

3. Select a WordArt style from the WordArt gallery and click OK.

4. Enter the WordArt text.

5. Select a font style, size, and font options.

6. Click OK to insert the WordArt object.

7. With the WordArt object selected, set formatting options for the object:
   - Choose Format→WordArt, select the options you want on the Colors And Lines tab, and click OK, or
   - Click the Format WordArt button on the WordArt toolbar, select the options you want on the Colors And Lines tab, and click OK, or
   - Click the various formatting buttons on the Drawing toolbar (Fill Color, Line Color, Line Style, and so on) to set each option individually.

> You can also use the Format→WordArt dialog box to set other common properties for WordArt, such as Size and Layout.

8. Use the sizing handles on the WordArt object to change the size and shape of the object as desired.

ACTIVITY 6-2

Inserting WordArt

Setup:
My Burke Graphics is open.

Scenario:
You want to create an unusual look for the "Burke Properties" title for the document. You don't think you can accomplish the effects you want just by using font formatting options.

What You Do	How You Do It
1. Used the arched WordArt style to insert and center the title "Burke Properties" at the top of the My Burke Graphics document.	a. On the vertical scroll bar, **click the Previous Page button** to move to the top of the first page of the document.
	b. On the Drawing toolbar, **click the Insert WordArt button**.

c. **Select the arched WordArt style** (the third option from the left in the top row).

Select a <u>W</u>ordArt style:

d. **Click OK** to display the Edit WordArt Text dialog box.

e. **Type** *Burke Properties*

f. **Click OK** to insert the WordArt object in the document.

g. On the Formatting toolbar, **click the Center button** to center the title.

2. **Set the fill color for the WordArt object to pale blue.**

a. **Click the WordArt object** to select it.

b. On the Drawing toolbar, **click the Fill Color arrow.**

c. **Click the Pale Blue fill color in the bottom row.**

d. **Save the document.**

TOPIC C

Insert Text Boxes

In Topic 6B, you used WordArt to insert text that you could treat as a graphic object. Another option for managing text as a graphic is to use a text box. In this topic, you will insert text boxes.

Text boxes are like the best of both worlds. You can treat them as graphics, and still use them to deliver fairly large quantities of text. You might have an announcement in a newsletter that has to stay on page one. You might need to add some commentary next to a chart. You might have some text that you need to fit inside a precise area of your document. Text boxes can meet your needs in all of these cases.

Text Boxes

Definition:

A *text box* is a graphic entity that serves as a container for text or for other graphics. Because the text box is a graphic object, it can be moved or sized. Text and graphics within the box move with the box. Text in the box flows to conform to the shape of the box. You can enter any text or graphics you need within the box and format the text or graphics as desired. You can also format the text box itself as you would format any other graphic object.

Example: A Text Box

Who We Are
Burke Properties is a full-service real estate brokerage firm. We provide a broad range of real estate services including residential and commercial sales and leasing. Jan Burke, the principal broker, has been personally involved in all phases of real estate for over 20 years. The brokers and associates of Burke Properties offer our clients a unique blend of specialties in the various markets within the area.

> More sales in the last 10 years than any other area broker!

Figure 6-3: *A text box.*

 A paragraph that is formatted with a border and shading may look like a large text box. However, you cannot move, size, rotate, or wrap other text around the paragraph as you can a text box.

How to Insert Text Boxes

Procedure Reference: Insert a Text Box

To insert a text box:

1. Place the insertion point where you want the text box to appear.

2. Choose Insert→Text Box or click the Text Box button on the Drawing toolbar.

3. Press Esc to remove the drawing canvas if you prefer to draw outside the canvas.

4. Drag to draw the text box. When you release the mouse button, the Text Box toolbar will appear.

5. Type the text you want in the box.

6. Select the text and use normal text-formatting procedures to set any text formatting properties you want.

7. If you want to change the orientation of the text in the text box, click the Change Text Direction button on the Text Box toolbar.

8. Set appearance, text wrapping, size, position, and any other properties for the text box as you would for any other graphic object. (To move the box, drag it by the box border to avoid moving the text inside the box.)

Activity 6-3

Inserting a Text Box

Setup:

My Burke Graphics is open.

Scenario:

Burke Properties has had more sales in the last 10 years than any other area real estate firm. You want to get that important message across to clients in an unusual way. It shouldn't look like just another paragraph.

What You Do	How You Do It
1. In My Burke Graphics, **insert a text box in the first paragraph.**	a. The first full paragraph of the document begins "Burke Properties is...." Place the insertion point at the beginning of the first full paragraph.
	b. On the Drawing toolbar, **click the Text Box button** 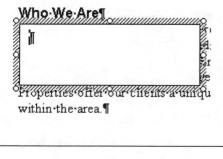 .
	c. **Press Esc to remove the drawing canvas.**
	d. **Drag to draw a text box that covers the first four lines of height and about one-third of the width of the first paragraph of text.**

2. Enter text in the text box.

    a. Type *More sales in the last 10 years than any other area broker!*

    b. On the Formatting toolbar, **click the Center button** to center the text in the box.

---

3. **Set the fill color for the text box to pale blue.**

    a. On the Drawing toolbar, **click the Fill Color arrow.**

    b. **Click the Pale Blue fill color in the bottom row.**

---

4. **Set the text wrapping style for the text box to square and centered.**

    a. **Choose Format→Text Box.**

    b. On the Layout tab, **click Square.**

    c. **Select Right.**

    d. **Click OK.**

    e. **Click in the first paragraph** to deselect and view the text box.

> **Who·We·Are¶**
> Burke·Properties·is·a·full-service·real·estate· brokerage·firm.·We·provide·a·broad·range·of· real·estate·services·including·residential·and· commercial·sales·and·leasing.·Jan·Burke,·the· principal·broker,·has·been·personally·involved· in·all·phases·of·real·estate·for·over·20·years.·The·brokers·and·associates·of·Burke· Properties·offer·our·clients·a·unique·blend·of·specialties·in·the·various·markets· within·the·area.¶
>
> More·sales·in·the·last·10·years· than·any·other·area·broker!¶

    📌 Feel free to adjust the size, shape, and position of the box.

    f. **Save the document.**

TOPIC D

Create Diagrams

Throughout this lesson, you've created and modified various types of individual graphic elements, such as shapes, lines, and text boxes. Common business diagrams, such as organization charts or Venn diagrams, combine a number of different simple graphic elements to create more complex structures. In this topic, you will create diagrams in Word.

It would be pretty hard to create a great-looking organization chart by drawing all the shapes, lines, and text boxes by hand. Word's dedicated diagramming tools help you build sharp, professional-looking business diagrams much more easily than you can with freehand drawing. Just specify the content and structure for the diagram, and leave the drawing to Word.

Types of Diagrams

You can insert six different types of standard business diagrams into a Word document.

Diagram Type	Use to Show
Organization Chart	Relationships between individuals and roles in an organization.
Cycle Diagram	A continuous process.
Target Diagram	Steps toward a goal.
Radial Diagram	Relationships of elements to a main element.
Venn Diagram	Areas of overlap between elements.
Pyramid Diagram	Relationships of elements to a foundation.

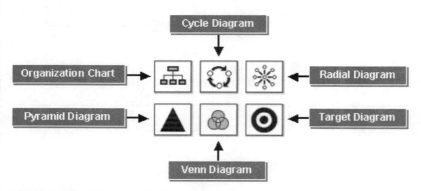

Figure 6-4: *The diagram gallery.*

Shape Types in Organization Charts

You can include four different shapes in organization charts to show different specific relationships between the various people and roles in the chart.

Shape Type	Appears on the Chart
Superior	Above and connected to other shapes.
Assistant	Below a superior shape, connected to it by an elbow (bent) connecting line, and above any subordinate shapes connected to the same superior shape.
Subordinate	Below a superior shape.
Coworker	On the same level as other shapes connected to the same superior shape.

How to Create Diagrams

Procedure Reference: Create an Organization Chart

An organization chart has specific elements that differ from other types of diagrams. To create an organization chart:

1. Insert an organization chart diagram into your document.
    - Click the Insert Diagram Or Organization Chart button on the Drawing toolbar and then select Organization Chart from the Diagram Gallery, or
    - Choose Insert→Picture→Organizational Chart.

    A basic organization chart containing one superior and three subordinate shapes appears in your document.

2. Click in each shape and type the text for the shape.

3. Delete shapes you do not need by right-clicking the shape and choosing Delete.

4. Add shapes as needed:
    a. Select the shape the new shape will be attached to.
    b. On the Organization Chart toolbar, click the Insert Shape drop-down arrow and select the type of shape you need.

5. Adjust the size of the organization chart as needed by clicking the Layout arrow on the Organization Chart toolbar and choosing an option:
    - Fit Organization Chart To Contents to automatically scale the chart to match your document.
    - Expand Organization Chart to incrementally increase the overall size of the chart.
    - Scale Organization Chart to add sizing handles to the chart so you can drag it to the correct size.

6. Adjust the appearance properties (fill color, line color, line style, and so on) for each shape on the organization chart as you would for other graphic objects.

> See the Microsoft Office Word Help system for information about advanced organization chart AutoFormat and Text Wrapping options available on the Organization Chart toolbar.

Procedure Reference: Insert a Diagram

You can use the following general steps to insert other types of diagrams into a document:

1. Display the Drawing toolbar.

2. Place the insertion point where you want to create the diagram.

3. Click the Insert Diagram Or Organization Chart button on the Drawing toolbar.

> You can use the toolbar button to insert all types of diagrams. You can use the Insert→Picture menu to insert an organization chart only.

4. In the Diagram Gallery, click the type of diagram you want to create and click OK. A basic diagram of that type appears, along with the Diagram toolbar.

5. Click Insert Shape on the Diagram toolbar to insert additional shapes into your diagram.

6. Click the Click To Add Text prompts and type the text you need to add to the diagram.

7. Adjust the shape, size, and appearance of the diagram.

Editing an Organization Chart

You can alter the contents of an organization chart at any time. Simply select the chart to activate it, and then select the chart elements you need to modify. A selected shape will have small round handles on the border of the shape.

ACTIVITY 6-4

Creating an Organization Chart

Setup:

My Burke Graphics is open.

Scenario:

You would like to add some information to your document about new client-service staff that Burke Properties has added. However, you don't think a simple list of names will add very much visual interest to the document.

What You Do	**How You Do It**
1. In My Burke Graphics, **insert a basic organization chart below the "We're Growing" section at the top of the second page.**	a. On the vertical scroll bar, **click the Next Page button** to move to the top of the second page of the document.
	b. **Place the insertion point on the first blank paragraph mark on the second page.**
	c. **Choose Insert→Picture→Organization Chart** to insert the basic organization chart.

2. Add the names and titles for Jan Burke and the three new Realtors: Roger Jones, Lucy Lambert, and Donna Gonzales.

a. Click in the shape in the top row.

b. Type *Jan Burke*

c. Press Enter.

d. Type *President*

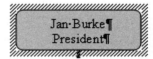

e. Click in the shape on the left of the second row.

f. Type *Roger Jones*

g. Press Enter.

h. Type *Realtor*

i. Click in the shape in the middle of the second row.

j. Type *Lucy Lambert*

k. Press Enter.

l. Type *Realtor*

m. Click in the shape on the right of the second row.

n. Type *Donna Gonzales*

o. Press Enter.

p. Type *Realtor*

3. Add an assistant shape with the information for Jan Burke's assistant, Molly Armitage.

a. Select the top shape (the shape for Jan Burke).

b. On the Organization Chart toolbar, **click the Insert Shape arrow and choose Assistant.**

c. In the new shape, **type** *Molly Armitage*

d. **Press Enter.**

e. **Type** *Realtor Assistant*

---

4. **Preview and save the document.**

a. On the Standard toolbar, **click the Print Preview button.**

b. **Press Page Up and Page Down** to view the graphics on both pages of the document.

c. On the Print Preview toolbar, **click the Close button.**

d. **Save and close the document.**

Lesson 6 Follow-up

In this lesson, you created a number of different customized graphic elements to use in your business documents. Being able to create your own graphics means that you don't have to depend on the pictures and Clip Art files that Word supplies by default; you have the ability to create the specific graphic element you need to suit your document.

1. **What kinds of documents have you seen that incorporate custom graphics?**

2. **Which of the custom graphic features you covered in this lesson do you think you will need to use?**

LESSON 7
Controlling Text Flow

Lesson Time
45 minutes

Lesson Objectives:

In this lesson, you will control text flow.

You will:

- Insert section breaks.
- Insert columns.
- Link text boxes.

Introduction

In this course so far, you've been creating and modifying various separate document elements. Now it's time to take a step back and consider the overall document flow. In this lesson, you will control text flow in your Word documents.

Documents don't always contain simple margin-to-margin text. Sometimes you need to break up the text or make it flow differently on the page. For an example, think of a departmental newsletter; you might want it to be laid out in two columns, with a banner headline spanning the columns. You might have two different stories that both start on page one and then continue on other pages of the document. These are the kinds of effects you can achieve by modifying a document's text flow.

TOPIC A

Insert Section Breaks

There are several techniques you can use to control the flow of text within a document. Section breaks enable you to set different document layout options for different portions of the same document. In this topic, you'll insert section breaks.

Section breaks come into play when you need different page layout options in different parts of the same document. For example, perhaps you need different margin widths on different parts of a single page. Or perhaps some pages need to print in landscape orientation, others to print in portrait orientation. Section breaks let you achieve all these effects.

Document Sections

Definition:

A *section* is a portion of a document that can have page layout options set independently from other portions of the document. *Section breaks* mark the boundaries between multiple sections in a document. Unlike page or column breaks, there are no automatic section breaks; to divide a document into multiple sections, you must insert section breaks manually. The type of the section break can vary. The page layout options applied to each different section can also vary.

Example: A Multiple-section Document

An annual report might contain a large table that cannot print on a single page in portrait layout. The table can be formatted as a separate section: that section can be formatted to print in landscape mode.

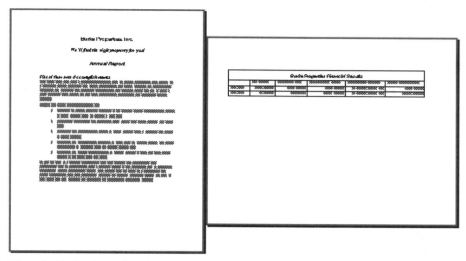

Figure 7-1: *A multiple-section document.*

Types of Section Breaks

There are four different section break types.

Section Break Type	Use When You Want the Next Section To
Next Page	Begin on a new page, as when you want to set different print output options for the section (paper source, size, or type, or page orientation, for example).
Continuous	Remain on the current page, as when you want one part of a page to have different margins than another part of the page.
Even Page	Start on an even-numbered (left-hand) page.
Odd Page	Start on an odd-numbered (right-hand) page.

How to Insert Section Breaks

Procedure Reference: Insert a Section Break

To insert a section break:

1. Place the insertion point just after the point of the break. (It helps to show non-printing symbols so you can select a specific paragraph mark.)

2. Choose Insert→Break.

3. Select the type of section break.

4. Click OK.

Activity 7-1

Inserting Section Breaks

Data Files:

- Newsletter.doc

Setup:

Word is set to show non-printing characters.

Scenario:

You've created a newsletter for Burke Properties, Inc. The newsletter has a table with the publication information, a blue-shaded masthead with the heading and subheading, and body text. As you review the newsletter, you find that the heading in the masthead is wrapping onto two lines. It would look better if there were room for this part of the heading to print on a single line.

What You Do	How You Do It
1. In the Newsletter document, **insert section breaks before and after the masthead.**	a. **Open Newsletter.**
	b. **Place the insertion point on the paragraph mark immediately before the blue-shaded masthead block.**
	This is the second empty paragraph mark after the "Volume A" table.
	c. **Choose Insert→Break.**
	d. **Under Section Break Types, select Continuous.**

	e. **Click OK.**
	f. **Place the insertion point on the second paragraph mark after the heading/ subheading block.**
	This is the empty paragraph mark right before the "About Us" text.
	g. **Insert a continuous section break.**

2. **How can you tell what section you are in?**

3. **Change the left and right margins for the banner heading to 1 inch each, and save the document as *My Newsletter*.**

a. **Position the insertion point anywhere in section 2 (between the two section breaks).**

b. **Choose File→Page Setup.**

c. **On the Margins tab, change the Left and Right margins to 1 inch.**

d. **In the Apply To drop-down list, verify that This Section is selected. Click OK.**

e. **With the new margins, the newsletter heading no longer wraps to two lines. Save the document as *My Newsletter***

TOPIC B

Insert Columns

Simple margin-to-margin text is a very common layout choice for many documents. However, another common option is to format the text so that it flows into multiple columns on a page. In this topic, you will insert columns into Word documents.

You can use columns in many different situations and with different types of documents. A newsletter is one document type that is often laid out in columns. If you have a long list with many short items, you can use columns to wrap the list to get more text on a page. Text formatting in columns can be easy on the eye because there is more white space on the page. Columns can help you meet these and other document layout needs.

How to Insert Columns

Procedure Reference: Insert or Format Columns by Using the Menu

Use the menu if you want to set formatting options for your columns. To create or format columns by using the menu:

1. Place the insertion point where you want the new columns to start, or inside existing columns you want to format.

2. Choose Format→Columns.

3. Set the number of columns:
   - Select a present column format, or
   - Enter the number of columns in the Number Of Columns text box.

4. Set the width and spacing for the columns:
   - Set a width and spacing value for each individual column, or

- Check Equal Column Width for balanced columns.

5. Check Line Between if you want to draw a vertical line between your columns.

6. From the Apply To drop-down list, select Whole Document, This Section, or This Point Forward. If you choose This Point Forward, Word inserts a section break before the new section of columns.

7. Check Start New Column if you want the text following the insertion point to move to the top of the next column. This choice is available if you chose This Point Forward.

8. Click OK.

Procedure Reference: Insert Columns by Using the Toolbar

You can create simple balanced columns quickly with the Columns toolbar button. To create columns by using the Columns toolbar button:

1. Place the insertion point where you want the columns to start.

2. Click the Columns button on the Standard toolbar.

3. Click the 1, 2, 3, or 4 column configuration. Word will create columns of equal width and with equal space between.

Procedure Reference: Insert Column Breaks

After you insert columns, you might find that the text does not wrap appropriately from one column to another. Just as you can insert page breaks to control where a new page will start, you can insert column breaks to control where a new column will start.

To insert column breaks:

1. Switch to Print Layout view to verify the current column breaks.

2. Place the insertion point just before the start of the new column.

3. Choose Insert→Break.

4. Select Column Break.

5. Click OK.

Paragraph Flow Options in Columnar Text

You can use standard paragraph flow settings, such as widow and orphan control, on text that is formatted in columns. For example, if you want two paragraphs always to appear in the same column, you can set the Keep With Next property on the first paragraph, just as you would with margin-to-margin text if you wanted the two paragraphs always to appear on the same page.

ACTIVITY 7-2

Inserting Columns

Setup:

My Newsletter is open.

Scenario:

After reviewing several sample publications from other firms, you realize that most of them use a two-column format. You want to be sure that if your publication uses columns, that it won't create any paragraph flow problems.

What You Do	How You Do It
1. In My Newsletter, **create a two-column layout with a separator line for the remainder document after the masthead.**	a. **Place the insertion point at the beginning of the About Us line.**
	b. **Choose Format→Columns.**
	c. In the Presets area, **click Two.**
	d. **Verify that Line Between is checked.**

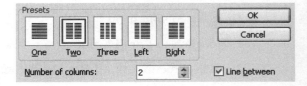

	e. From the Apply To drop-down list, **select This Point Forward.**
	f. **Click OK** to insert another section break and create the columns.

2. Break the columns so that the "Our New Web Site" title prints on the same page as the text that follows it.

  a. Scroll to the bottom of page 2.

  b. The "Our New Web Site" section title has become separated from the section text. **Place the insertion point at the beginning of the Our New Web Site line,** before the bullet character.

  c. **Choose Insert→Break.**

  d. **Select Column Break.**

  e. **Click OK** to wrap the Our New Web Site title and text together onto page 3.

3. Preview, save, and close the completed My Newsletter document.

  a. On the Standard toolbar, **click the Print Preview button.**

  b. **Press Page Up and Page Down** to view the document.

  c. On the Print Preview toolbar, **click the Close button.**

  d. **Save the document.**

  e. **Close the document.**

TOPIC C

Link Text Boxes

In Topic 7B, you controlled text flow by inserting columns. Another way to achieve a very similar text-flow effect is to link text boxes together. In this topic, you will link text boxes.

Columns in Word are newspaper-style, which means the text flows continuously from one column to another. You can't control exactly which column or which page your text will appear on. For example, you can't use columns to start an article on page 1 of a newsletter and continue it on page 3. For layout effects like this, you need linked text boxes. Use linked text boxes in documents like newsletters and reports to get professional-quality layout options for your documents.

How to Link Text Boxes

Procedure Reference: Link Text Boxes

To link text boxes:

1. Select Print Layout view.

2. Insert the text boxes that you want to link at the locations you want them in your document.

3. Click the border of the first text box to select it.

4. Type or paste text into the first text box.

5. Display the Text Box toolbar.

6. Click the Create Text Box Link button on the Text Box toolbar 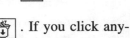 .

   The mouse pointer will change to an icon of a full pitcher . If you click anywhere other than on a text box, or if you press Esc, you will cancel the link operation.

7. Click in the second text box to link the first text box to it. The mouse pointer will appear as a pouring pitcher icon before you click .

8. Adjust the size, shape, and appearance of the text boxes as necessary.

Adding Text After Linking

You can also add text to the text boxes after you have linked them together.

Breaking a Link

To remove a text box from the linked chain, click the box and click the Break Forward Link button on the Text Box toolbar.

ACTIVITY 7-3

Linking Text Boxes

Data Files:

- Newsletter Box.doc
- Rates Text.doc

Scenario:

You are working on a newsletter for Burke Properties, Inc. Most of the newsletter has been laid out and formatted in columns. The managing broker for your office has provided you with a separate document that contains the text for a fairly lengthy article on mortgage rates. You know this will be interesting to your clients and you want to feature the article prominently, without taking up too much space on page 1.

What You Do	How You Do It
1. Copy and paste the article text from the Rates Text document into the text box on page 1 of Newsletter Box.	a. **Open Newsletter Box.**
	b. **Press Page Down twice** to view the first text box, at the bottom of the first column on page 1.
	c. The article will begin on page 1 and will finish at the end of the newsletter. **Press Page Down four times** to move to the last page and view the column break.
	d. **Press Page Up four times** to return to the text box on page 1.
	e. **Open Rates Text.**
	f. **Choose Edit→Select All.**
	g. **Choose Edit→Copy.**
	h. **Close Rates Text.**
	i. In Newsletter Box, **click in the text box on page 1.**
	j. **Choose Edit→Paste** to insert the text into the text box. The text will overflow the box.

2. In Newsletter Box, **draw the text box for the continuation of the article on page 3.**

a. **Place the insertion point on the blank paragraph mark at the top of the second column on page 3.**

   🖈 This is right after the paragraph that reads "continued from page 1."

b. On the Drawing toolbar, **click the Text Box button.**

c. **Press Esc** to close the drawing canvas.

d. **Drag to draw a text box that is slightly taller and wider than the table in the adjacent column.**

3. **Link the text boxes.**

a. **Press Page Up several times** to move to the text box on page 1.

b. **Click in the text box on page 1** to select it.

c. On the Text Box toolbar, **click the Create Text Box Link button** .

📌 If the Text Box toolbar is not open, choose View→Toolbars→Text Box to display it.

d. The mouse pointer now resembles a full pitcher. **Press Page Down four times** to move to the text box on page 3.

⚠️ Use the keyboard to scroll. Do not click anywhere, or you will cancel the link operation.

e. When the mouse is above the text box on page 3, the mouse pointer resembles a pouring pitcher. **Click the text box on page 3** to link it to the first text box.

(continued from page 1)¶
¶
7.0%;·15-year·fixed·mortgages·are·at· 6.875%;·and·1-year·adjustable·rate· mortgages·are·at·6.2%.¶
¶
For·this·month,·the·30-year·mortgage·rate·is· one·percent·lower·than·one·year·ago,· according·to·information·released·by·the· Mortgage·Market·Information·Services,·a· mortgage·report·recording·service.¶
¶

📌 If you want, you can adjust the size and shape of the text box slightly.

4. **Preview the document.**

a. **Click the Print Preview button.**

b. **Scroll through the document.**

c. **Close Print Preview.**

5. **Save the completed newsletter as** *My Newsletter Box* **and close the document.**

    a. **Save the document as** *My Newsletter Box*

    b. **Close the open document.**

Lesson 7 Follow-up

In this lesson, you used several different techniques to control the overall flow of text in a document. With these techniques, you can adjust the overall look of any portion of your document to make sure text appears where you need it to be and how you need it to look.

1. **What types of business documents have you seen that incorporate any of the text-flow options in this lesson?**

2. **Which of the text-flow control options do you think you will be using the most in your documents?**

LESSON 8
Automating Common Tasks

Lesson Objectives:

In this lesson, you will automate common tasks.

You will:

- Run a macro.
- Create a macro.
- Modify a macro.
- Customize toolbars and buttons.
- Add menu items.

Introduction

One of the goals of this course is to help you become a more efficient user of Word. One way to improve your efficiency is to automate tasks that you perform on a regular basis. In this lesson, you will automate common Word tasks.

As a proficient Word user, you may begin to find that there are tasks that are specific to your own work flow that you perform over and over again. Perhaps you apply the same custom paragraph style frequently. Perhaps you create the same customized headers or footers. Perhaps you often set the same text wrapping properties on a picture you've inserted. It would be nice to perform those specialized tasks at the touch of a button. This lesson will show you how to automate the tasks you perform every day and get more work done in less time.

TOPIC A

Run a Macro

This lesson covers various ways to automate common tasks in Word. The primary tool that you will use to automate tasks is the macro. In this topic, you'll run macros to perform tasks automatically.

There may be tasks that you do over and over again that are specific to your own work environment. For example, maybe everyone in your company sets up a standard business letter in the same way. Many companies create and distribute macros so that employees can perform these tasks quickly and consistently. If you have job-specific macros available in your work environment, knowing how to run them successfully can be a great time-saving tool.

Macros

Definition:

A *macro* is a set of Word commands and instructions grouped together as a single command. Each macro is uniquely identified by a macro name. Macros consist of programming code that provides the instructions for the macro commands. A macro can perform any repeatable combination of Word commands. Macros can be stored in documents or in templates.

Example: A Find and Replace Macro

You are a copy editor for your state government's Department of Environmental Conservation. You're responsible for making sure that the agency's name always appears in print in a consistent format. Staff members in the department commonly submit text that includes several different common variations on the agency name: "Environmental Conservation Department," "Department of the Environment," "Department of Conservation and the Environment," and so on. Rather than scanning each document to locate and update each one of these incorrect instances, you use a macro that runs Word's Find and Replace feature several times to automatically make all the different corrections with a single command.

Macro Security

Because macros contain programming code, they have the potential to produce harmful effects on your system. These effects can be caused inadvertently, by improper macro construction. Or, they can be caused deliberately, if the macro writer uses the macro code as a delivery method for malicious programs such as computer viruses. To reduce the risk of unsafe macros, Microsoft has constructed a macro security system that enables you to disable macros that are potentially unsafe. A disabled macro cannot run, which means that unsafe code in the macro cannot execute, thus protecting your system. Macros are enabled or disabled when you open the document or load the template that contains the macros.

The macro security system incorporates various elements.

- *Trusted publishers*. These are individuals or organizations whose macros you deem safe.

- *Digital signatures*. This is a small amount of electronic code included with a macro to identify the publisher of the macro. You cannot trust the publisher of a macro that is not digitally signed.

- *Macro security levels*. This is the Word setting that determines how Word will handle macros that are not from trusted publishers.

You can view or change the macro security level on the Security Level tab of the Security dialog box. Choose Tools→Macro→Security. There are three macro security levels.

Security Level	Word's Actions when Opening a Document Containing Macros
High	Automatically enables macros from trusted publishers; automatically disables unsigned macros. For signed macros from publishers not on the trusted list, provides the option to add the publisher to the list.
Medium	Automatically enables macros from trusted publishers. For unsigned macros, prompts user to enable or disable the macros. For signed macros from publishers not on the trusted list, provides the option to add the publisher to the list.
Low	Automatically enables all macros. Use this setting only if you have a separate virus-scanning program or some other local security system in place.

You can view the Trusted Publishers list on the Trusted Publishers tab of the Security dialog box. You can also use this tab to remove publishers from the list.

How to Run a Macro

Procedure Reference: Run a Macro

To run an existing macro:

1. Open the document where you are going to run the macro.

2. Click Enable Macros if you are prompted to enable or disable macros in the document.

3. Choose Tools→Macro→Macros to open the Macros dialog box.

4. Select the name of the macro you want to run. By default, all macros in all active documents and templates are listed.

5. Click Run.

ACTIVITY 8-1

Running a Macro

Data Files:

- Burke Name Change.doc

Setup:

The macro security level has been set to Medium. The NameChange macro has been added to the Normal template in Word.

Scenario:

Burke Properties has recently changed and trademarked the company name. All company literature, both internal and external, needs to be updated with the new trademarked name. The technical support team has created and distributed a macro that automates this process, but each employee is responsible for running the macro on individual documents.

What You Do	How You Do It
1. Examine the company names in the Burke Name Change document.	a. Open Burke Name Change.
	b. Press Page Down to scroll and view the company names in the document.
2. How does the company name appear in the document?	
3. Run the NameChange macro and save the document as *My Name Change*.	a. Choose Tools→Macro→Macros.

b. With the NameChange macro selected, **click Run** to run the macro.

c. **Press Page Down** to view the company names in the document.

d. **Save the document as** *My Name Change*

4. How does the company name now appear in the document?

TOPIC B

Create a Macro

In Topic 8A, you ran macros that had already been created. You can also create your own personalized macros. In this topic, you will create macros in Word.

What tasks do you personally do over and over? Perhaps you search for and replace the same text frequently, add a standard header or footer, or insert the date using a specific format. No matter what the task, if can you do it by repeating the same keystrokes or mouse clicks, you can create a macro to do it for you.

How to Create a Macro

Procedure Reference: Record a Macro

To record a macro:

1. Plan the sequence of steps and commands you want the macro to perform.

2. Determine any keyboard shortcuts you will need to record to substitute for specific mouse movements (such as selecting text).

3. Perform the steps you plan to record at least once before you start recording. This is to verify:

   • The macro will produce the desired result.

   • The macro will not depend on the specific content in the current document.

   • The macro will not depend upon specific mouse movements. For example, you cannot use the mouse to select text, as this depends on the specific position of the mouse. Use keyboard alternatives for selecting text.

4. Open a document.

5. Open the Record Macro dialog box:

    -   Double-click the gray REC indicator on the status bar REC .

    -   Choose Tools→Macro→Record New Macro.

    -   Display the Visual Basic toolbar and click the Record Macro button ⊙ .

6. Enter a name for the macro in the Macro Name text box.

    ✐ If you want, you can assign the macro to a keyboard shortcut or toolbar button, but this is optional.

7. Select a location for the macro from the Store Macro In drop-down list. By default, the macro will be stored in the Normal template and will be available to all documents, but you can also choose to store the macro in the current document.

8. Enter an optional description for the macro in the Description text box.

9. Click OK. The Stop Recording toolbar is displayed. The mouse pointer will appear with a miniature tape recorder icon attached.

10. Perform the steps in the macro.

    As you record, you can click the Pause Recording/Resume Recording button to pause and resume recording if you need to omit some keystrokes.

11. Stop the recording:

    -   Click the Stop Recording button on the toolbar, or

    -   Double-click REC on the status bar.

12. Run the macro to test it. If the macro is stored in the Normal template, test it in a new document.

Macro Naming Rules

There are several rules to follow when you create macro names.

-   The name must begin with a letter.
-   The name must not contain spaces.
-   The name can contain letters, numbers, and the underscore character.

The Stop Recording Toolbar

The Stop Recording toolbar contains two buttons: Stop Recording and Pause Recording.

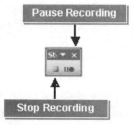

Figure 8-1: *The Stop Recording toolbar.*

ACTIVITY 8-2

Recording a Macro

Setup:

My Name Change is open.

Scenario:

While Burke Properties has provided everyone with a macro to change the company name in all documents, you would also like to add a custom footer, containing the company name and the page number, to the documents that you personally create. It is time-consuming to create this footer by hand in each document.

What You Do	How You Do It
1. You need to plan your macro. What are the general steps you must take to create the macro?	
2. Does this macro require that you record mouse movements?	
3. Create and name the new BurkeFooter macro.	a. Choose Tools→Macro→Record New Macro.
	b. In the Macro Name text box, **type BurkeFooter**
	c. In the Store Macro In list box, **verify that the macro will be stored in All Documents (Normal.dot).**
	d. **Select the text in the Description text box.**
	e. In the Description text box, **type *Creates standard document footer*.**
	f. **Click OK** to display the Stop Recording toolbar and begin recording.
	The mouse pointer now has a small cassette-tape icon attached. The REC indicator on the status bar is bold, not gray.

Lesson 8

4. **Record the macro to include the company name at the right and the current page number to the left.**

a. Choose View→Header And Footer.

b. On the Headers And Footers toolbar, **click the Switch Between Header And Footer button** .

c. **Type** *Burke Properties*

d. You need to include the trademark sign to be consistent with the company standards. **Choose Insert→Symbol.**

e. In the Recently Used Symbols list, **select the trademark symbol.**

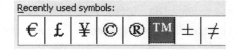

f. **Click Insert** to insert the trademark symbol into the footer.

g. **Click Close.**

h. **Press Tab twice** to move to the right-aligned section of the footer.

i. **Type** *Page*

j. **Press Spacebar.**

k. On the Headers And Footers toolbar, **click the Insert Page Number button** .

l. On the Headers And Footers toolbar, **click the Close button** Close .

m. On the Stop Recording toolbar, **click the Stop Recording button** .

n. **Save the document.**

5. **Test the macro.**

    a. **Open a new, blank document.**

    b. **Run the BurkeFooter macro.**

    c. **Press Page Down twice** to scroll to the bottom of the page and verify the appearance of the new footer.

    d. **Close the new document without saving changes.**

TOPIC C

Modify a Macro

In Topic 8B, you created a macro. You can also modify an existing macro if you need to make small changes to its functionality. In this topic, you will modify macros.

Suppose you have a macro that you use to start business letters. It inserts and formats your company's name and address and a standard business greeting. Then suppose that your company name changes because of a merger. You need to change the contents of that macro. You could re-record the macro from scratch, but why? It's working fine—why risk making a typo in a new macro? In cases like this, it's more efficient to make a small modification to the existing macro than it is to start again from scratch.

Visual Basic for Applications (VBA)

Visual Basic for Applications (VBA) is the programming language used to create macros in Microsoft Office 2003 applications. When you record a macro, Word automatically translates the keystrokes and commands into VBA code language, and creates and stores the macro.

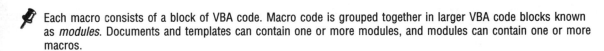 Each macro consists of a block of VBA code. Macro code is grouped together in larger VBA code blocks known as *modules*. Documents and templates can contain one or more modules, and modules can contain one or more macros.

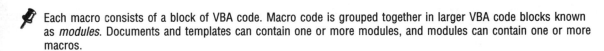 If you have a knowledge of VBA programming language and syntax, you can write macros directly in VBA.

The Visual Basic Editor Window

The Visual Basic Editor is an add-in application you can use to load, view, and edit the VBA code for a macro. When you load a macro for editing, it appears in the Visual Basic Editor window, which has its own interface, menu bar, and Help system. The Visual Basic Editor window contains several components.

Visual Basic Editor Window Component	Description
Project Explorer	A hierarchical interface listing the VBA modules in all open documents and templates. The normal template is listed as "Normal." Open documents appear as "Project" objects. Open templates appear as "TemplateProject" objects.
Properties Window	Lists the properties of whatever item is selected in the Project Explorer. A property is a characteristic of the item. For example, one property of a VBA module is the module's name.
Code Window	Displays the VBA code for the selected project for editing.

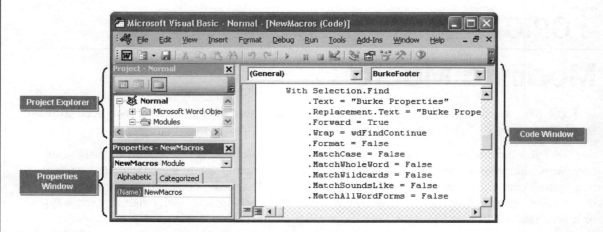

Figure 8-2: *The Visual Basic Editor window.*

For more information on VBA and the Visual Basic Editor, see the Visual Basic Help system.

 If you have experience with Microsoft Office Excel 2003, you might also be interested in the Element K course "Excel 2003: Introduction to VBA."

How to Modify a Macro

Procedure Reference: Modify a Macro

To modify a macro:

1. Open the document where the macro is stored, or that uses the template where the macro is stored.

2. Choose Tools→Macro→Macros.

3. Select the macro and click Edit.

4. Edit the VBA code for the macro in the Visual Basic Editor window.

5. Choose File→Close And Return To Microsoft Word.

6. Test the macro.

ACTIVITY 8-3

Modifying a Macro

Setup:

My Name Change is open.

Scenario:

A new corporate communications guideline just issued by Burke Properties requests all employees to use the company's tag line in conjunction with the company's name wherever possible. You think you can accomplish this by including the tagline in your standard footer.

What You Do	How You Do It
1. In My Name Change, **open the BurkeFooter macro for editing.**	a. **Choose Tools→Macro→Macros.**
	b. BurkeFooter is first in the list, and selected by default. **Click Edit** to open the Visual Basic Editor window and display the code that runs the BurkeFooter macro.
2. **Add the tagline text, "We'll find the right property for you!" in the centered position in the footer text.**	a. **Double-click the title bar of the code window** to maximize the window for easier scrolling.
	b. The second `Selection.TypeText` command line inserts the two tab characters and the page number information. **Click to place the insertion point right before the second vbTab code in this line.**
| | ```
Selection.TypeText Text:=vbTab & vbTab
``` |
| | c. Including the quotation marks, **type "*We'll find the right property for you!*"** and press Spacebar. |
| | d. **Type & and press Spacebar** again. |
```

e. Verify that there is a space, an ampersand, and another space between the new text and the second **vbTab** code character.

```
for you!" & vbTab
```

f. Choose File→Close And Return To Microsoft Word.

g. Save My Name Change.

3. **Test the macro in a new document.**

a. **Open a new, blank document.**

b. **Run the BurkeFooter macro.**

c. **Scroll to the bottom of the page** to verify the appearance of the new footer.

d. **Close the new document without saving changes.**

4. **How could you update the footer in the current document?**

TOPIC D
Customize Toolbars and Buttons

In the first three topics of this lesson, you created and ran macros by using the Macros dialog box. An alternative, quicker way to access macros and other types of commands is to attach them to toolbar buttons. In this topic, you will customize toolbars and buttons to run your own custom commands.

OK, you have some great macros that automate various tasks for you. But you have to open up the Macros dialog box to run each one! With so many keystrokes, sometimes you think that you need a macro to run your macros. Well, not quite—what you really need in this situation is your own custom toolbar buttons, to give you one-click access to your favorite macros and other commands.

How to Customize Toolbars and Buttons

Procedure Reference: Create a Custom Button

To create a custom button on a toolbar:

1. Display the toolbar to which you will add the custom button.

2. Open the Customize dialog box:
   - Choose Tools→Customize, or
   - Right-click a menu or toolbar and choose Customize.

3. Select the Commands tab.

4. Select a category of commands from the Categories list. For macro commands, select the Macros category.

5. Select the command from the Commands list.

6. Drag the command from the Commands list outside the Customize box and to the position on the toolbar where you want to attach it. (The I-beam mouse pointer shows you where the new button will appear on the toolbar.)

7. Click Modify Selection if you want to change the button.
   - Enter a new name for the button in the Name text box.
   - Select an image to attach to the button from the Change Button Image palette.
   - Select a button style:
     — Default Style for the image only.
     — Text Only (Always)
     — Text Only (In Menus)
     — Image And Text

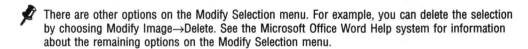 There are other options on the Modify Selection menu. For example, you can delete the selection by choosing Modify Image→Delete. See the Microsoft Office Word Help system for information about the remaining options on the Modify Selection menu.

8. Repeat steps 4 through 7 for any other buttons you want to create.

9. Click Close in the Customize dialog box.

Procedure Reference: Create a Custom Toolbar

If you want to attach buttons to a custom toolbar, you will need to create the toolbar first. To create a custom toolbar:

1. Open the Customize dialog box.

2. Select the Toolbars tab.

3. Click New.

4. Enter a name for the toolbar in the Toolbar Name text box.

5. From the Make Toolbar Available In drop-down list, select the document or template where you want to store the toolbar.

6. Click OK. The new toolbar will appear.

7. Select the Commands tab and add commands to the toolbar.

8. Click Close to close the Customize dialog box when you have finished adding commands.

Assigning a Macro to a Button While Recording

You can assign a macro to a button as you record the macro. In the Record Macro dialog box, click the Toolbars button to open the Customize dialog box and follow the steps for creating a button.

Removing Custom Buttons and Toolbars

To remove a custom toolbar, on the Toolbars tab of the Customize dialog box, select the toolbar, and click Delete. To remove a custom button, open the Customize dialog box and drag the button off the toolbar.

Resetting Toolbars and Buttons

You can reset all menus, toolbars, and buttons to their Word system defaults. Open the Customize dialog box. On the Options tab, click the Reset Menu And Toolbar Usage Data button and click Yes. On the Toolbars tab, click Reset. Click OK.

ACTIVITY 8-4

Creating a Custom Toolbar Button

Setup:
My Name Change is open.

Scenario:
You are using your custom BurkeFooter macro more than you ever expected. You use it at least as often as you use some of the buttons on the Standard toolbar, for example. You wish that it was as easy to run the macro as it is to access the commands on the visible toolbars.

What You Do	How You Do It
1. With My Name Change open, **assign the BurkeFooter macro to a new button to the left of the Print Preview button on the Standard toolbar.**	a. **Choose Tools→Customize.** b. **Select the Commands tab.** c. **Scroll down in the Categories list** to display the Macros category.

d. In the Categories list, **select Macros.**

e. In the Commands list, **select the BurkeFooter macro.**

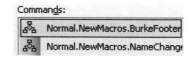

f. **Drag the BurkeFooter macro to the left of the Print Preview button on the Standard toolbar** to add the button to the toolbar with default button text.

---

2. **Modify the default button appearance to include descriptive text reading "BurkeFooter" and an image of footsteps.**

a. In the Customize dialog box, **click Modify Selection.**

b. **Click in the Name text box** to select the text.

c. **Type *BurkeFooter***

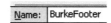

d. On the Modify Selection menu, **click Change Button Image.**

e. In the Change Button Image gallery, **click the image of footsteps.**

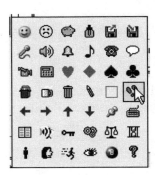

f. In the Customize dialog box, **click Close** to verify that the button appears on the toolbar with your custom image and text.

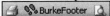

Procedure Reference: Add or Remove Standard Buttons

You cannot delete standard toolbars, but you can add or remove standard buttons from the standard toolbars. To add or remove a button:

1. On the toolbar that you want to modify, click Add Or Remove Buttons.

2. If a submenu appears, choose the toolbar you want to modify.

3. Check a button you want to add; uncheck a button you want to remove.

4. Click in the Word window to close the menus.

OPTIONAL DISCOVERY ACTIVITY 8-5

Removing a Standard Button

Scenario:
Now that you've added your custom button to the Standard toolbar, you think the toolbar looks a little busy. On the other hand, you never use the Hyperlink button on that toolbar.

---

1. **Remove the Hyperlink button from the Standard toolbar.**

     You can add the button back at any time.

TOPIC E

Add Menu Items

In Topic 8D, you customized toolbars and buttons to run your custom commands. Another, similar way to access the commands you use frequently is to create customized menu items. In this topic, you will add menu items to run your personalized commands.

Adding customized menu items can make your work more efficient by saving you time and keystrokes. No more drilling through layers of menus for the one command you need. No more "losing" menu choices because you can't remember what submenu they are in. Custom menu items put the commands you use most frequently only one or two clicks away.

How to Add Menu Items

Procedure Reference: Create a Custom Menu

To create a custom menu:

1. Open the Customize dialog box and select the Commands tab.

2. From the Categories list, select New Menu.

3. Drag New Menu from the Commands list to the menu bar.

4. Use Modify Selection to enter a descriptive name for the new menu.

5. Drag the command you want to the new menu. Release the command over the drop-down area that appears when you point to the new menu. The command will be added as a submenu item.

6. Use Modify Selection to enter a descriptive name for the new submenu item.

7. Repeat steps 5 and 6 for each additional command you want to add.

8. Close the Customize dialog box.

 You might choose to create custom menus rather than custom toolbar buttons if you want to be able to access your custom commands using the keyboard. Creating a menu also saves screen space by enabling you to group commands together under a single command.

Removing a Custom Menu

You can remove a custom menu in the same way that you remove a custom button. Open the Customize dialog box and drag the item off the menu bar.

ACTIVITY 8-6

Creating a Custom Menu

Setup:

My Name Change is open.

Scenario:

You expect to create several more macros in the future. You want to be able to access the macros quickly, but you don't want to have so many separate buttons taking up space on your toolbar.

What You Do	How You Do It
1. **Create a new main menu item to the left of the Help menu.**	a. **Open the Customize dialog box.**
	b. On the Commands tab, in the Categories list, **scroll to display the New Menu category** (at the bottom of the list).
	c. **Select New Menu.**
	d. From the Commands list, **drag the New Menu command to the menu bar between the Window menu and the Help menu.**

2. **Name the new menu Macros.**

   a. In the Customize dialog box, **click Modify Selection.**

   b. **Click in the Name text box** to select the text.

   c. **Type** *Macros*

   d. **Click the Modify Selection button** to close the menu.

---

3. **Add the BurkeFooter macro as a submenu on the new Macros menu.**

   a. In the Categories list, **select Macros.**

   b. From the Commands list, **drag the BurkeFooter macro to the drop-down area below the new Macros menu.**

---

4. **Name the new submenu Burke Footer.**

   a. In the Customize dialog box, **click Modify Selection.**

   b. **Click in the Name text box** to select the text.

   c. **Type** *Burke Footer* to name the new submenu.

   d. **Click the Modify Selection button** to close the menu.

   e. In the Customize dialog box, **click Close.**

   f. **Click the Macros menu** to display the Burke Footer submenu.

   g. **Save and close My Name Change.**

Lesson 8 Follow-up

In this lesson, you learned how to use macros to automate common tasks. If you can run, record, and modify macros, you can use these powerful tools to automate any repetitive task that you perform now, saving yourself time and ensuring your accuracy.

1. In what ways have you seen macros used in your work environment?

2. What repetitive tasks do you perform now that you think you might automate with a macro?

LESSON 9

Automating Document Creation

Lesson Objectives:

In this lesson, you will automate document creation.

You will:

*   Create a document based on a template.
*   Create a document by using a wizard.
*   Create or modify a template.
*   Change the default template location.
*   Insert a MacroButton field in a template.

Introduction

In Lesson 8, you learned about methods to improve your work efficiency by automating a variety of tasks. Another way to increase your efficiency is to automate the process of document creation itself. In this lesson, you will automate the creation of Word documents.

A standard business document is like a puzzle; you put together pieces such as styles, standard text, specific layout, and graphics options to complete the final effect. If you create the same kinds of business documents frequently, you don't need to put those pieces together by hand every time. You can use Word features to put together the key pieces of the document's structure and format automatically.

TOPIC A

Create a Document Based on a Template

This lesson covers various ways to automate the process of creating a document. One common way of automating document creation is to base a new document on a specific template. In this topic, you'll create a document by basing it on a template.

Templates can automate the basic setup steps when starting a new document—setting up the margins, choosing the styles, planning the general layout, and roughing out the main document content. If you use a template to do these generic tasks, it will free up your time and energy so that you can concentrate on the content that's specific to your document. Select the right template as a basis for your document, and you'll feel as if the document is half done as soon as you start it.

Template Locations

There are two main locations where you can find templates to use as a basis for new documents.

- *The local computer.* A default installation of Word includes many locally installed templates. These templates are listed in the Templates dialog box.

- *The Internet.* Microsoft makes many templates available on its Web site. There is a link to this site in the New Document task pane.

Template File Locations

Template files are stored in various locations on your local computer. They can also be stored on a local network.

- *The installed templates location.* By default, Word places locally installed templates on the drive where Windows is installed, in the path \Program Files\ Microsoft Office\Templates\1033.

- *The default user template location.* This is the folder where the Normal.dot template is located. Each user on a system has a separate default template location and separate version of Normal.dot. By default, it will be on the drive where Windows is installed, in the path \Documents And Settings\(username)\Application Data\Microsoft\Templates. Any other templates stored in this location will also appear in the Templates dialog box.

- *The downloaded templates location.* If you base a document on a template that is stored on the Internet, Word will download a copy of the template to your local computer, on the drive where Windows is installed, in the path \Documents And Settings\(username)\Local Settings\Temp.

- *The workgroup templates location.* The local network administrator can place templates in a network location.

How to Create a Document Based on a Template

Procedure Reference: Create a Document Based on a Template

To create a document based on a template:

1. Choose File→New to open the New Document task pane.

    > Do not click the New Document button if you want to choose your template. This creates a new document based on the Normal template.

2. Select the template you want to use:
    - To search for a template on Microsoft.com, enter a search term in the Search text box.
    - To browse for a template on Microsoft.com, click the Templates Home Page link, and then click links to the various template categories.
    - To browse for a template stored on the local computer, click the On My Computer link to open the Templates dialog box.

3. Open a document based on the template:
    - On the Microsoft Templates Web site, click the Edit In Microsoft Word button for the template you want.
    - In the Templates dialog box, click the template and then click OK.

4. Edit the default text in the template as needed.

5. Save the document.

The Attached Template

When you base a document on a template, the template is attached to the document. As you edit the document, you can access the styles, macros, and other elements in the attached template.

You can view or change the attached template by opening the document and choosing Tools→Templates And Add-Ins. The path and name of the currently attached template will appear in the Document Template text box. Click Attach to change the attached template.

When you change the attached template, the current contents of the document do not change, but you can now access the styles, macros, and other elements in the new template when you edit the document in the future.

ACTIVITY 9-1

Creating a Document Based on a Template

Scenario:

You're Heather LaPierre, a property manager at Burke Properties. Jan Burke, the president of Burke Properties, is vacationing in Hawaii and you are handling some of her duties in her absence. Today, you met with Bob Wannamaker from the Creative Associates ad agency. During the meeting, you and Bob made handwritten changes to some new ad copy. You want to fax the changes to Jan for her approval, and you want to include a professional-looking cover sheet.

What You Do	How You Do It
1. **Open a new document based on the Professional Fax template.**	a. **Choose File→New.** The New Document task pane opens.
	b. Under Templates, **click On My Computer** to open the Templates dialog box.
	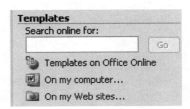
	c. **Click the Letters And Faxes tab.**
	d. **Click the Professional Fax template.**
	e. **Click OK** to open a new document based on the template for editing in Word.

2. **Edit the default template text in the document to include the To, From, and CC names, the number of pages, and Jan's fax and phone numbers (808-555-1111 and 808-555-2222).**

The date in the fax template is generated by a date and time field in Word, so it will always display the current date.

a. The generic "Click here and type return address..." text at the top of the document is generated by the template. **Click on the text that reads "Click here and type return address..." to select it.**

b. **Press Delete.**

c. The "Company Name Here" text is actually a one-cell table. **Select the "Company Name Here" text.**

d. **Type** *Burke Properties*

Burke Properties¤

e. The To and From area of the template is also a table. **Click the generated text on the To: line.**

f. **Type** *Jan Burke* to replace the generated field text with your own text.

g. **Select the text on the From line and type** *Heather LaPierre*

h. On the Fax line, **enter** *808-555-1111*

i. On the Pages line, **enter** *2 total*.

j. On the Phone line, **enter** *808-555-2222*

k. On the Re line, **enter** *Ad meeting notes*

l. On the CC line, **enter** *Bob Wannamaker, Creative Associates*

To:¤	Jan·Burke¤	From:¤	Heather·LaPierre¤
Fax:¤	808-555-1111¤	Pages:¤	2·total¤
Phone:¤	808-555-2222¤	Date:¤	3/21/2003¤
Re:¤	Ad·meeting·notes¤	CC:¤	Bob·Wannamaker,·Creative·Associates¤

m. **Scroll down and select the text that follows the word Comments**

n. **Enter** *Let us know what you think.*

3. Save the document as *My Fax* and close the document.

   a. Save the document as *My Fax*

   b. Close the document.

TOPIC B

Create a Document by Using a Wizard

In Topic 9A, you created documents by basing them on selected templates. A wizard is another type of document-creation tool that uses templates. In this topic, you'll create a document by using a wizard.

You know that choosing an appropriate template for your document can do a lot of the basic document setup work for you. Using a wizard can take this process of automation one step further. Not only does the wizard create the look and structure for your document, but it can also help guide you through entering some of the custom content you'll need. There are wizards that produce a wide variety of standard business documents; take a look and see if there might just be a wizard for you.

Document Wizards

Definition:

A *document wizard* is a miniature application that uses a multi-page format to guide a user through the process of creating standard business documents. Document wizards are listed on the various pages of the Templates dialog box. A document wizard uses a series of prompts to gather the basic information needed to complete a document based on a selected template.

Example: The Resume Wizard

The eight pages of the Resume Wizard prompt you to select a resume template and organizational structure (for example, chronological) for the resume, and to insert your name, address, and the headings you want to use in the resume.

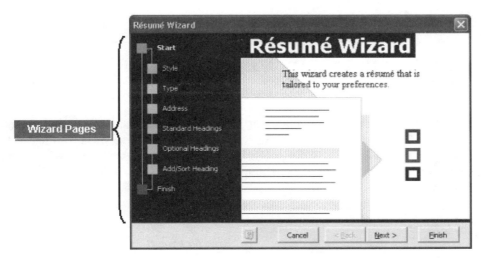

Figure 9-1: *The Resume Wizard.*

How to Create a Document by Using a Wizard

Procedure Reference: Create a Document by Using a Wizard

To create a document by using a wizard:

1. Choose File→New to open the New Document task pane.

2. In the New Document task pane, click the On My Computer link to open the Templates dialog box.

3. In the Templates dialog box, click the wizard you want to use and click OK. A wizard will run and prompt you for the information you need to complete the template on which this wizard is based.

4. Fill in the information on each page of the wizard and click Next.

5. Click Finish when you are done. Word creates a document that contains your information and settings.

6. Edit the document further as necessary.

7. Save the document.

ACTIVITY 9-2

Creating a Document by Using a Wizard

Scenario:

You're Heather LaPierre, a property manager at Burke Properties. Jan Burke, the president of Burke Properties, is vacationing in Hawaii and you are handling some of her duties in her absence. Today, you met with Bob Wannamaker from the Creative Associates ad agency. During the meeting, you and Bob made handwritten changes to some new ad copy. You want to fax the changes to Jan for her approval, and you want a quick and accurate way to create a professional-looking cover sheet.

What You Do	How You Do It
1. Run the Fax Wizard.	a. Choose File→New.
	b. Under Templates, **click On My Computer** to open the Templates dialog box.
	c. On the Letters & Faxes tab, **click the Fax Wizard.**
	 Fax Wizard
	d. **Click OK** to run the Fax Wizard.
2. **Complete the Fax Wizard with Jan's name and fax number (808-555-1111) and your name.**	a. On the first page of the Fax Wizard, **click Next.**
	b. You are faxing a hard copy, not an electronic document. **Verify that Just A Cover Sheet With A Note is selected and click Next.**
	c. **Select I Want To Print My Document So I Can Send It From A Separate Fax Machine. Click Next.**
	d. In the first Name text box, **type** *Jan Burke*

e. In the first Fax Number text box, **type 808-555-1111 and click Next.**

f. **Verify that Professional style is selected and click Next.**

g. On the Who Is The Fax From? page, in the Name text box, **type *Heather LaPierre* and click Next.**

h. **Click Finish to create the basic fax.**

3. **Save the document as *My Fax Wizard* and close the document.**	a. **Save the document as *My Fax Wizard***
	b. **Close the document.**

TOPIC C

Create or Modify a Template

In the first two topics of this lesson, you created documents based on existing templates. You can also customize templates to meet your own particular needs. In this topic, you will create or modify templates so that you can include custom elements.

Creating your own custom template gives you an easy, consistent way to incorporate your own custom elements into new documents. It might be your own electronic letterhead, sections of standardized text, or a consistent set of formats. If the built-in Word templates don't exactly meet your needs, create one for yourself to get the precise results you need for your documents.

How to Create or Modify a Template

Procedure Reference: Create or Modify a Template Based on a Document

To create or modify a template based on a document:

1. Create or open the document you will base the template on.

2. Make any necessary changes to the document.

3. Choose File→Save As.

4. From the Save As drop-down list, select Document Template. Word automatically changes the Save In location to the default Word templates location. This means that your template will be available as a choice on the General tab in the Templates dialog box.

5. If you want the template to appear on a different tab of the Templates dialog box, place it in a subfolder within the Templates folder.

6. Specify a file name:
   - For a new template, enter a unique name for your template.
   - For an existing template, select the existing template name.

7. Click Save. If you are modifying an existing template, confirm that you want to replace the existing template file.

8. Test the template by opening a new document based on the template.

Basing a Template Directly on a Template

You can choose to base a template directly on another template. When you select a template in the Templates dialog box, select the Template radio button under Create New to open a new template file for editing.

Using a Document as a Template

You can use any Word document as a template. Any document files stored in the Word default template location will appear as choices in the Templates dialog box.

ACTIVITY 9-3

Creating a Template

Data Files:
- Burke Fax.doc

Scenario:
As a property manager for Burke Properties, you often send fax cover sheets to accompany contracts and other documents you transmit to clients by fax. You have been using a standard Word fax template to create the cover sheets, and you wish you could quickly create other similar cover sheets that have some of the same standard information you've been entering each time by hand.

What You Do	How You Do It
1. **Remove Jan Burke's name and fax number, the number of pages, and the Comments text from the Burke Fax document so you can use it as the basis for a template.**	a. **Open Burke Fax.**
	b. This fax document was personalized in various ways. On the To line, **drag to select Jan Burke's name.**
	c. **Press Delete** to delete Jan Burke's name from the To line.
	d. **Delete Jan Burke's fax number.**
	e. **Delete the number of pages.**
	f. **Delete the text in the Comments paragraph.**
	Leave the Comments heading.
2. **Save the edited document as a template called *My Template*.**	a. **Choose File→Save As.**
	b. From the Save As Type drop-down list, **select Document Template.**
	c. In the File Name text box, **enter *My Template***
	d. **Verify that the save location has changed to the Word default template location and click Save.**

	e. **Close My Template.**

3.   **Test the template.**

a.   **Choose File→New.**

b.   **Under Templates, click On My Computer.**

c.   **Select the General tab** to verify that the new My Template appears.

d.   **Click My Template and click OK** to open a new document based on your template.

e.   **Close the new document without saving changes.**

Procedure Reference: Change the Default Font in the Normal Template

Microsoft provides a direct way to alter the font in the Normal template. To change the default font in the Normal template:

1.   Open a document based on the Normal template.

2.   Choose Format→Font.

3.   Select the options you want.

4.   Click Default.

5.   Click Yes to verify that you want to change the default font for the Normal template.

6.   Test the change by opening a new document based on the Normal template.

ACTIVITY 9-4

Changing the Default Font

Scenario:

Burke Properties has changed its corporate communications standard to state that all company documents should use Arial, 12 pt, as the base font. You want to make this change globally on your system so that you don't have to remember to change the font settings each time you open a new document.

What You Do	How You Do It
1. Change the default font in the Normal template.	a. **Click the New Blank Document button** to create a new, blank document based on the Normal template.
	b. **Choose Format→Font.**
	c. From the Font list, **select Arial.**
	d. **Click Default.**
	e. **Click Yes** to confirm that you want to update the Normal.dot template.
	f. **Close the new, blank document without saving changes.**
2. Test the template changes.	a. **Click the New Blank Document button** to create a new document based on the Normal template.
	b. On the Formatting toolbar, **verify that Arial appears in the Font text box and close the new document without saving changes.**

TOPIC D

Change the Default Template Location

In Topic 9C, you stored custom templates in Word's default template location. If you choose, you can store your templates in a different location. In this topic, you'll change the default template location so that you can access your custom templates from a different storage location.

If you create and use a lot of your own templates, you might find it easier to manage them if you store them separately from the Word templates. You might even want to create your own categories for the templates so that you can find them easily in the Templates dialog box. Word enables you to do this simply by changing the default template file location. By changing the default template location, you can merge your own personal templates right in with Word's built-in ones. So, no matter where you store your templates, you can easily access your own templates, as well as Microsoft's, from the Templates dialog box.

How to Change the Default Template Location

Procedure Reference: Change the Default Template Location

To change the default template location:

1. Move or copy the template files to the folder you want to use as the template location.

2. Place templates in subfolders within this folder if you want to categorize your templates.

3. Open any document.

4. Choose Tools→Options.

5. Select the File Locations tab.

6. In the File Types list, select User Templates.

7. Click Modify.

8. Browse to select the new template location.

9. Click OK in the Modify Location dialog box.

10. Click OK in the Options dialog box. Word copies the Normal template to the new default location.

11. Verify the new location by opening the Templates dialog box. The General tab of the Templates dialog box should show the templates in the new default location, along with the other default Word templates. If you have templates in subfolders in the new default location, the subfolders will appear as additional tabs in the Templates dialog box.

ACTIVITY 9-5

Changing the Default Template Location

Data Files:

- Custom Templates\Burke Fax Template.dot

Setup:

The Burke Fax Template.dot template file is stored in the My Documents\Custom Templates folder for your user account.

Scenario:

You have created a number of custom templates and stored them in your My Documents folder in a subfolder called Custom Templates. You need to be able to access these templates from the Templates dialog box.

What You Do	How You Do It
1. **Change the default template location.**	a. **Open a new, blank document.**
	b. **Choose Tools→Options.**
	c. **Select the File Locations tab.**
	d. In the File Types list, **select User Templates.**
	e. **Click Modify** to open the Modify Location dialog box and display the current template folder.
	f. On the My Places bar in the Modify Location dialog box, **click My Documents.**
	g. There is a subfolder in My Documents called Custom Templates. **Double-click the Custom Templates folder.**
	h. There is a template in this folder called Burke Fax Template.dot, but the template file is not visible because the Modify Location dialog box does not display files, only folders. **Click OK.**
	i. The new template location appears in the File Types list. In the Options dialog box, **click OK.**

2. **Verify the new default template location.**

    a. **Choose File→New.**

    b. **Click On My Computer.**

    c. Burke Fax Template appears as a choice on the General tab. **Click Burke Fax Template and click OK** to open a new document based on the template in Word.

    d. **Close the new document without saving it.**

Topic E

Insert a MacroButton Field in a Template

In Topic 9C, you saw that customized templates can contain document elements such as AutoText entries, fonts, key assignments, macros, menus, page layout, special formatting, and styles. Templates can also contain various types of fields to assist you in adding text to documents based on the template. In this topic, you will insert a MacroButton field into a template.

A custom template that contains styles, formatting, page layout, and default text elements goes a long way towards helping you create great-looking documents quickly. But the templates that Microsoft provided with Word don't only include text and formatting; they actually guide you when you create a document because they include a special field which not only describes the text you need for the document, but also gives you one-click replacement of the standard text in the template. Well, you don't have to work for Microsoft to get this kind of functionality. You can use the MacroButton field to get that same one-click text replacement function in your own custom templates.

Field Codes

Fields are automatically updating sections of a document. Fields contain programming instructions called *field codes* that tell Word how to determine the results of the field. Word normally displays the results of the field in the document, not the field codes.

Field Code Syntax

All field codes follow the same basic syntax.

```
FIELD NAME arguments "field text" /switches
```

- The field name is the basic function the field performs. For example, when you insert the current page number in a document, you insert a field named PAGE

- The arguments are any information that is required for the field to return a result. If there are spaces in an argument, it is enclosed in quotes. For example, if you insert the "Yours truly," autotext entry as a field, you would provide the name of the entry as an argument. The field code would appear as: AUTOTEXT "Yours truly,"

- The field text is text that is displayed to the user in the field result. Field text is enclosed in quotes. For example, if you insert the document author's name as a field, you could include the author's name as field text: AUTHOR "Nancy Curtis"

- Switches are any number of variables that can be used with the field to control the field results. Available switches vary from field to field. For example, a Page field in a footer will have a format switch to indicate the number format used. PAGE *Arabic would produce a page number with an Arabic numeral.

 One case in which you might use field codes to insert text, such as the author's name, instead of typing the text, is when you are including the field in a macro. For example, you might create a macro that inserts several different fields of information about a document in a document footer. Each user who ran the macro would get customized text.

Revealing Codes

There are several ways to see the codes for fields in a document:

- Right-click a field and choose Toggle Field Codes to reveal the code for that field.
- Select a field and press Shift+F9 to reveal the code for that field.
- Press Alt+F9 to reveal all codes in a document.

Available Word Fields

To see a list of the fields available in Word and the individual syntax for each field, choose Insert→Field. Individual descriptions and Help for each field are available in the Microsoft Office Word Help system.

The MacroButton Field

The MacroButton field is a Word field that is often used in templates. It provides automatic prompts for the template user, and one-click replacement of template text.

The MacroButton Field Syntax

The syntax of the MacroButton field is: MacroButton MacroName DisplayText where MacroName is the macro to run and DisplayText is the text that will appear in the document where you insert the field. A user can run the attached macro by double-clicking the display text.

For one-click selection and replacement of boilerplate text in a template, use the NoMacro argument instead of a macro name. Your boilerplate text is the DisplayText. For example, you could insert the field MacroButton NoMacro "Click here and enter your name" in a letter template to prompt a user to type his or her name at the end of the document.

ACTIVITY 9-6

Examining the MacroButton Field Codes

Scenario:

You're interested in building a template that includes some of the functionality of Word's built-in templates. Before you begin, you want to examine the coding in a built-in Word template that you've used before, the Professional Fax template.

What You Do	How You Do It
1. **Open a document based on the Professional Fax template.**	a. **Choose File→New.**
	b. **Under Recently Used Templates, click Professional Fax.**
2. **Examine the codes in the MacroButton fields in the document.**	a. **Press Alt+F9.** This template contains several MacroButton fields. These fields both describe the text you should enter at that point in the document, and provide for one-click replacement of the description text with your custom text.
	To:※　{MACROBUTTON·NoMacro·[Click·**here**·and·type·name]}※
	b. **Press Alt+F9** to hide the field codes again.
	c. **Close the new document without saving changes.**

How to Insert a MacroButton Field in a Template

Procedure Reference: Insert a MacroButton Field in a Template

To insert a MacroButton field in a template:

1. Open the template, or a document based on the template, for editing.

2. Place the insertion point where you want the MacroButton fields to appear.

3. Choose Insert→Field.

4. In the Field Names list, select MacroButton.

5. Click Field Codes to open a text box where you can edit the field codes directly.

6. Edit the text in the Field Codes text box to read MACROBUTTON NoMacro You are creating a button that does not have a macro attached to it.

7. After the MACROBUTTON NoMacro entry, enter a space, and type the placeholder text that you would like to appear in the document.

8. Click OK.

9. When you have finished entering the fields, save the document as a template.

10. Test the codes in the template by opening a new document based on the template.

11. Click once on any MacroButton field to select the entire text of the field.

OPTIONAL ACTIVITY 9-7

Inserting MacroButton Fields in a Template

Data Files:

- Custom Templates\Burke Fax Template.dot

Scenario:

You've created a customized fax template to use at Burke Properties. However, when you look at some of the pre-supplied Word templates, you realize that your custom template would be even easier to use if it prompted the user for the text to supply in each area of the document.

What You Do	How You Do It
1. Open a document based on the Burke Fax Template template for editing.	a. Choose File→New.
	b. Under Recently Used Templates, click **Burke Fax Template.**

2. **Insert a MacroButton field for the recipient's name.**

a. **Place the insertion point in the cell next to the word To.**

b. **Choose Insert→Field.**

c. **In the Field Names list, scroll down and select MacroButton.**

Field names:
IncludePicture
IncludeText
Index
Info
Keywords
LastSavedBy
Link
ListNum
MacroButton
MergeField
MergeRec
MergeSeq
Next
NextIf
NoteRef

Description:
Run a macro

d. **Click Field Codes.**

e. In the Field Codes text box, **enter**

   MACROBUTTON NoMacro [Recipient's Name]

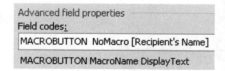

Advanced field properties
Field codes:
MACROBUTTON NoMacro [Recipient's Name]
MACROBUTTON MacroName DisplayText

f. **Click OK.**

3. Enter MacroButton fields for the recipient's fax number and the number of pages.

   a. Click in the Fax line and choose Insert→ Field.

   b. In the Field Names list, **scroll down and select MacroButton.**

   c. **Click Field Codes.**

   d. In the Field Codes text box, **enter**

      MACROBUTTON NoMacro [Recipient's Fax]

   e. **Click OK.**

   f. Using a similar procedure, in the Pages line, **insert a MacroButton field with the text *[Number of Pages]***

4. **Save the document as a new template.**

   a. **Choose File→Save As.**

   b. From the Save As Type drop-down list, **select Document Template.**

   c. In the File Name text box, **enter *My Fax Codes***

   d. **Verify that the Save location is the Custom Templates folder and click Save.**

   e. **Close My Fax Codes.**

5. **Test the template changes.**

    a. **Choose File→New.**

    b. **Click On My Computer** to open the Templates dialog box.

    c. The My Fax Codes template appears on the General tab. **Select My Fax Codes and click OK.**

    d. **Click the words {Recipient's Name}** to select the entire field.

    e. **Type** *Gina Lee* to replace the placeholder text automatically.

    f. **Close all open documents without saving changes.**

Lesson 9 Follow-up

In this lesson, you used a variety of tools to automate and streamline the process of document creation. Using these tools helps you set up great-looking documents quickly, with consistent results every time.

1. **For what types of business documents do you think you will find templates or wizards useful?**

2. **What elements do you think you might need to include in a custom template?**

LESSON 10
Performing Mail Merges

Lesson Time
50 minutes

Lesson Objectives:

In this lesson, you will perform mail merges.

You will:

- Examine the steps in the mail merge process.
- Perform a merge on existing documents.
- Merge envelopes and labels.
- Create a data source in Word.

Introduction

People who use word processing on a regular basis commonly need to produce documents, such as form letters, that are generally similar but customized for individual recipients. Word's mail merge feature enables you to create this type of document. In this lesson, you'll perform mail merges to produce a variety of customized documents.

Mail merge is a great tool if you need to produce a lot of similar documents that need just a little bit of customization. Maybe you personalize cover letters to include with each customer's billing statement. Maybe you run labels for bulk mailings. Maybe you work in an academic setting, and need to produce grade and score reports for individual students. Instead of creating each one of these documents individually, you can use a mail merge to produce them all in a few simple steps.

TOPIC A

The Mail Merge Process

There are several steps to a successful mail merge, and each step requires different components. Before performing a merge, you should understand the process you will follow. In this topic, you'll examine the steps in the mail merge process.

Before you start on a car trip, you probably get yourself a road map. And before you start to perform a mail merge, you should be able to map out the steps in the merge for yourself. If you understand the steps and components in the mail merge process before you start, you'll have a road map that will help you perform all types of merges successfully.

Mail Merge

You can use *mail merge* to combine static information in one document with variable information in another document. The merge produces multiple customized documents that share a basic structure. You can use mail merge in Word to create a wide variety of customized documents, including letters, emails, envelopes, labels, or even a company phone book.

 If you have seen a sweepstakes letter from a magazine publisher, you have seen the results of a mail merge.

The Main Merge Document

Definition:

The *main merge document* is the merge component that contains the text and formatting that does not vary in the final output. The main document must also contain one or more *merge fields*, which serve as placeholders for the variable merge information.

Example: A Main Merge Document

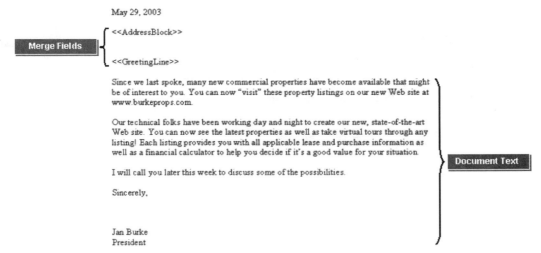

Figure 10-1: *A main merge document.*

The Data Source

Definition:

The *data source* is the merge component that contains the variable information for the merge. The data source must contain a row of field names followed by rows of information that contain the information for the fields.

Data Sources

The data source can be any one of a number of document types, such as a table in a Word document; an address list from Microsoft Outlook; or an Excel spreadsheet. Word supports the following file types as data sources:

- A Microsoft Outlook Contacts list.
- Address books from other email clients.
- An Office Address List (a list that you type during the merge process).
- A table in an Excel worksheet. The worksheet can contain multiple data source tables, each on a separate sheet.
- A table in an Access database.
- Tables in other databases.
- A table in an HTML file (a Web page file).
- A table in a Word document. The table must contain a header row with the field names, and data rows containing the merge data.
- A *delimited text file*. This is a plain text file in which the fields in each row are separated by a comma or tab character, and each row of data is separated by a carriage return. The first line in the file must contain the field names.

Example: A Data Source Document

Field Names →	FirstName	LastName	Address	City	State	Zip
	William	Davis	561 Third St.	Austin	TX	78701
Field Information	Julia	Nicholson	777 Garcia Ave.	Washington	DC	20001
	Carol	Smith	209 Parrish St.	Eugene	OR	97401
	Ben	Willenbecher	87 Country Lane	Charlottesville	VA	22901

Figure 10-2: *A data source document.*

The Mail Merge Process

The mail merge process involves:

1. Entering text and formatting the main document.
2. Creating the data source.
3. Inserting fields in the main document to link it to the data source.
4. Merging the information to produce the customized output.

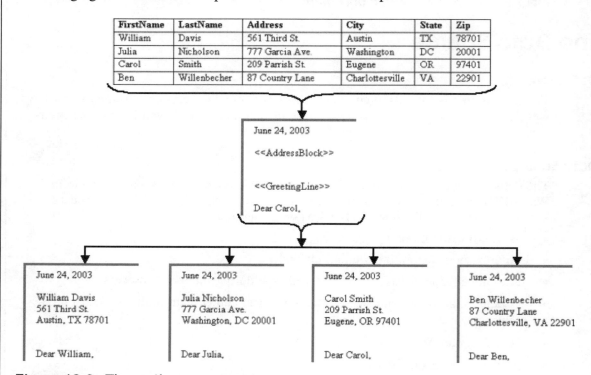

Figure 10-3: *The mail merge process.*

Merge Fields

You can insert any of the following merge fields into your main document:

Field Type	Field Name (Field Code)	Description
Merge field	Address Block (AddressBlock)	Inserts name and address information from the data source to create an address. Word will either automatically determine which fields in the data source contain the name and address, or will prompt you to match the fields manually.
Merge field	Greeting Line (GreetingLine)	Inserts the name of the recipient from the data source to create a greeting. Word will automatically determine which fields in the data source contain the name, or prompt you to match the fields manually.
Merge field	Electronic Postage (no field code)	Adds postage to mailings if an electronic postage program is installed.
Merge field	Postal Bar Code (BarCode)	Inserts a postal bar code based on street address and ZIP code information in the data source. Word will automatically determine which fields in the data source contain the address information, or prompt you to match the fields manually.
Database field	Varies according to field name in data source	Inserts content from a specified field in a data source.
Other mail merge fields	Various	Introduce programmatic logic into the mail-merge process. One example is the "Skip Record If (SkipIf)" field. See the Word Help system for more information on advanced Word fields.

ACTIVITY 10-1

Examining the Mail Merge Process

Data Files:

- Merge Letter.doc
- Mailing List.xls
- Complete Merge.doc

Scenario:

You're a Burke Properties agent in New York State. All agents in the company have been asked to send a form letter out over Jan Burke's signature to prospective commercial-property customers in each territory. Jan's assistant has already created the form letter and a company-wide mailing list. You're not sure what to do next, so you ask a more experienced agent for some help. She's sent you her merge documents to look over.

What You Do	How You Do It
1. Examine the Merge Letter form letter.	a. Open Merge Letter.
	b. After you have answered the following questions, **close the document without saving changes.**
2. What do you need to insert into this document to convert it to a main merge document?	
3. After you complete the merge, where should the variable information appear in this letter?	

4. **Use Microsoft Excel to examine the Mailing List data source spreadsheet.**

   a. **Click Start.**

   b. If you are using Windows 2000 Professional, **click Documents.**

   c. **Click My Documents.**

   d. **Select Mailing List.xls.**

   e. The data source file is not a Word document but an Excel spreadsheet. You cannot open it directly in Word. **Choose File→Open** to open Microsoft Excel and the Mailing List spreadsheet.

   f. After you have answered the following questions, **close Microsoft Excel.**

   g. **Close the My Documents folder.**

5. **How many fields are there in this data source? What are the fields?**

6. **What order do the rows appear in?**

7. **True or False? The data source contains rows of information only for customers in New York State.**

   ___ True

   ___ False

8. **Examine the Complete Merge document containing the completed merged letters.**

   a. In Word, **open Complete Merge.**

   b. **Press Page Down** to scroll through the document.

   c. After you have answered the following questions, **close the document without saving changes.**

9. **What two merge fields were inserted into the main merge document to link it to the data source?**

10. **Recipients from which states are included in this merged mailing?**

11. In what order do the mail merge letters appear?

TOPIC B

Perform a Merge on Existing Documents

In Topic 10A, you examined the steps in the merge process. Now that you understand the steps, you can put them together by performing a merge. In this topic, you'll perform a merge using existing documents.

Mail merge is a simple idea, but the process of performing a merge can be tricky. The information in this topic will enable you to perform successful merges every time, and produce stacks of great-looking customized documents in a fraction of the time it would take you to create each one by hand.

How to Perform a Merge on Existing Documents

Procedure Reference: Merge Existing Documents with the Mail Merge Task Pane

Microsoft provides a Mail Merge task pane to take you through all of the merge steps. To merge existing documents with the Mail Merge task pane:

1. Open a document:
   - Open a blank document, or
   - Open the document you plan to use for your main document.

   🖈 Although it is possible to create the main document and the data source as you perform a merge, it is generally preferable to create the documents ahead of time to be sure that they are structured correctly.

2. Choose Tools→Letters And Mailings→Mail Merge to open the Mail Merge task pane.
   - The Mail Merge task pane will open at Step 1 if you have a blank document open, or if Word cannot determine the merge document type.
   - The Mail Merge task pane will open at Step 3 if you have an existing main merge document open and Word can determine the document type.

3. If Step 1 is displayed, select one of the five document type options and click Next: Starting Document to move to Step 2.

4. Select the main document:
   - Select Use The Current Document if you have an existing main merge document open.

- Select Start From A Template if you need to create a new main merge document.

- Select Start From Existing Document to select an existing document from a list of files.

5. Click Next: Select Recipients to move to Step 3.

6. Select the data source:

   - Select Use An Existing List to use a Word, Excel, or Access data file as the data source.

   - Select Select From Outlook Contacts to use an Outlook email contacts list as a data source.

   - Select Type A New List only if you do not have an existing data source.

   The data source entries will appear in the Mail Merge Recipients dialog box.

7. Sort the data source, if desired:

   - To perform a one-level sort, click the desired column heading. Text fields will be sorted alphabetically from A to Z; number fields will be sorted numerically from lowest to highest.

   - To perform a multiple-level sort:

     1. Click the drop-down arrow next to any field name.

     2. Click Advanced to open the Filter And Sort dialog box.

     3. Select the Sort Records tab.

     4. Specify the sort fields and sort order.

     5. Click OK.

8. Filter the data source, if desired:

   - To perform a simple filter, click the drop-down arrow next to any field name and select an option:

     — All to show all recipients.

     — Blanks to show only recipients with blank information in that field.

     — Nonblanks to show only recipients with information in that field.

   - To perform an advanced filter:

     1. Click the drop-down arrow next to any field name.

     2. Click Advanced to open the Filter And Sort dialog box.

     3. Select the Filter Records tab.

     4. Select the field you want to filter by.

     5. Select the comparison operator.

     6. Enter the value you want to filter by.

     7. Click OK.

   You can create multiple filters by specifying AND or OR conditions. AND conditions exclude more records; OR conditions include more records. See the Microsoft Office Word Help system for more information.

9. Uncheck the check boxes for any individual recipients you want to exclude.

10. Click OK in the Mail Merge Recipients dialog box.

11. Click the Next field to move to Step 4. (For example, if you are writing a letter, click Next: Write Your Letter.)

12. Insert merge fields into the document:

    a. Position your insertion point where you want the field to appear.

    b. Select the field:

       • Click a standard merge field (such as AddressBlock or GreetingLine), or

       • Click More Items to insert fields directly from your data source. Select the field name and click Insert, and then click Close.

    > ✏ If the Match Fields dialog box appears, Word might not be able to map the standard merge field to the fields in your data source. Use the dialog box to select the correct fields.

    c. For standard merge fields, use the dialog box for the field to make any changes to the default settings for that field.

    d. Click OK in the dialog box for the field to insert the field.

    e. Repeat as necessary for other merge fields.

13. Click the Next field to move to Step 5. The data is merged together.

14. Preview the output for each recipient by clicking the Next and Previous buttons. As you preview, you can:

    • Exclude a selected recipient by clicking the Exclude This Recipient button.

    • Modify the recipient list by clicking Edit Recipient List.

15. Click Next: Complete The Merge to move to Step 6.

16. Print the completed document, if desired:

    a. Click Print.

    b. Select the records to print and click OK.

    c. Click OK in your printer's Print dialog box.

17. Save the completed document, if desired:

    a. Click Edit Individual Letters.

    b. Select the records to save and click OK to create a new document containing the selected records.

    c. Save the new document.

> ✏ You might save the merge output if you want to print it at a later time, or if you want to make customized edits to the output for specific recipients.

Saving the Main Document and Resuming a Merge

At any time during your merge, you can save the original main merge document. This will save the inserted merge field codes and a link to the data source, along with the document contents. You might do this if you want to resume the merge process at a later time. When you open the main merge document after saving it, Word will also open the associated data source. You can then open the Mail Merge task pane and complete the merge.

If Word cannot locate the data source, Word will prompt you to open the data source manually. If you do not want to open the data source or resume the merge, you can click Options. You can then click:

- Remove Data/Header Source to break the link between the two documents but leave the merge codes. Do this if you want to merge a different data source into this main document.

- Remove All Merge Info to remove the merge field codes and convert the document back to an ordinary Word document. Do this if you no longer need to use this document as the basis for a merge.

The Mail Merge Toolbar

You can also perform merges by using the Mail Merge toolbar. The buttons for each of the merge steps appear on the toolbar in order from left to right.

ACTIVITY 10-2

Merging Existing Documents

Data Files:

- Merge Letter.doc
- Mailing List.xls

Scenario:

You need to create personalized letters for the commercial-property customers in your New York State territory. You want to arrange the completed letters in a logical order. You are on a first-name basis with all of your customers. As you create the letters, you realize you are already closing a commercial-property deal with one customer, Elizabeth Milko.

What You Do	How You Do It
1. **Select Merge Letter as the main merge document.**	a. With a blank document open, **choose Tools→Letters And Mailings→Mail Merge** to open the Mail Merge task pane.
	b. **Verify that Letters is selected and click Next: Starting Document** to advance to the Step 2 Mail Merge task pane.
	c. **Select Start From Existing Document.**
	d. **Click Open.**
	e. **Open Merge Letter.** The main document opens in the document window.

2. **Select Sheet 1 of the Mailing List workbook as the data source.**

a. **Click Next: Select Recipients** to move to the Step 3 Mail Merge task pane.

b. **Verify that Use An Existing List is selected and click Browse.**

c. The default location for data sources is the My Data Sources subfolder. **Select the My Documents folder.**

d. **Open Mailing List.xls.**

e. In the Select Table dialog box, **click OK** to open Sheet 1 of the Excel workbook and display the data source data in the Mail Merge Recipients dialog box.

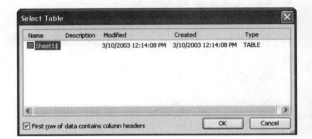

3. **Sort the data source by recipients' last name, and filter the data source to include only customers in New York State.**

a. In the Mail Merge Recipients dialog box, **click the LastName column heading** to sort the list alphabetically by last name.

 Click the words in the heading, not the drop-down arrow.

b. **Click the drop-down arrow next to the State column heading.**

c. You will use the advanced Filter and Sort features to produce letters to clients who live in New York State only. **Select (Advanced).**

d. In the Filter And Sort dialog box, on the Filter Records tab, **click the Field drop-down arrow.**

e. **Scroll down in the field list and select State.**

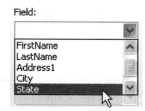

f. The comparison operator is automatically set to Equal To, creating an exact match with the field contents. In the Compare To text box, **enter NY**

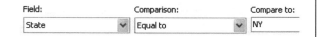

g. **Click OK.**

h. The filtered list shows five clients with addresses in New York State. In the Mail Merge Recipients dialog box, **click OK.**

4. **Insert the address block with no title and no company name.**

   a. **Click Next: Write Your Letter** to move to the Step 4 Mail Merge task pane.

   b. In the document, **place the insertion point on the second empty paragraph mark after the date.**

   c. Under Write Your Letter, **click Address Block** to open the Insert Address Block dialog box and display the default address settings.

   d. From the Insert Recipient's Name In This Format list, **select the choice for first and last name with no title.**

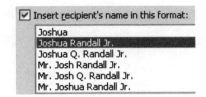

   e. **Uncheck Insert Company Name.**

   f. **Click OK** to insert the AddressBlock field in the letter.

```
March 10, 2003¶
¶
«AddressBlock»¶
¶
```

---

5. **Insert the greeting field with a first-name greeting.**

   a. **Position the insertion point on the third empty paragraph mark after the Address Block field.**

 There will be an empty paragraph mark after the greeting line and before the body of the letter.

   b. **Click Greeting Line.**

c. In the Greeting Line Format area, from the middle drop-down list, **select the first name greeting,** not the nickname greeting.

Greeting line format:

Dear | Joshua

d. **Click OK** to insert the GreetingLine field into the main document.

March·10,·2003¶
¶
«AddressBlock»¶
¶
¶
«GreetingLine»¶
¶

---

6. **Exclude Elizabeth Milko as a recipient.**

a. **Click Next: Preview Your Letters** to move to the Step 5 Mail Merge task pane.

b. **Click the Next Recipient button four times** [>>] to preview all the letters.

c. **Click the Previous Recipient button two times** to return to the letter for Recipient 3, Elizabeth Milko.

d. **Click Exclude This Recipient.**

---

7. **Print the completed letters.**

a. **Click Next: Complete The Merge** to move to the Step 6 Mail Merge task pane.

b. **Click Print** to open the Merge To Printer dialog box.

c. **Verify that All is selected and click OK** to open the Print dialog box.

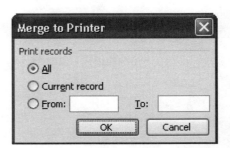

d. **Click OK** to send the letters to the default printer.

8. Save the individual letters as *My Mail Merge* and close the document.

a. Click **Edit Individual Letters** to open the Merge To New Document dialog box.

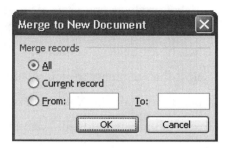

b. In the Merge To New Document dialog box, **verify that All is selected and click OK.**

c. The new document contains each separate letter on its own page. **Save the new document as *My Mail Merge***

d. **Close My Mail Merge.**

e. **Close the Mail Merge task pane.**

f. **Close the open main document without saving changes.**

TOPIC C

Merge Envelopes and Labels

In Topic 10B, you merged data to create a customized letter. You can also perform merges that create customized envelopes and labels. In this topic, you will merge envelopes and labels.

You've probably already realized that performing a mail merge is the fastest and easiest way to create any quantity of mailing labels or envelopes. With a simple main merge document and a data source for the addresses, it's easy to use the merge function to create and print as many envelopes and labels as you need.

How to Merge Envelopes and Labels

Procedure Reference: Merge Labels

To merge labels:

1. Open a blank document.

2. Open the Mail Merge task pane, select Labels, and click Next: Starting Document.

3. Click Label Options to specify a size for the labels. You can select from a variety of label products and sizes. The default is Avery 2160. Click OK. The document is now formatted as a sheet of labels.

4. Click Next: Select Recipients.

5. Select the recipients as you would in any mail merge.

6. Click Next: Arrange Your Labels.

7. Insert the merge fields into one of the labels on the page.

8. Scroll down in the Mail Merge task pane and click Update All Labels to copy the merge fields to the other labels.

9. Preview, save, or print your merged envelopes as you would in any mail merge.

Creating Labels by Hand

If you want to print a single label, choose Tools→Letters And Mailings→Envelopes And Labels and select the Labels tab. Enter the address into the text box, select Single Label, and click Print.

ACTIVITY 10-3

Merging Labels

Data Files:

• Mailing List.xls

Setup:

You have a print driver installed and configured as your default printer. You might or might not have a physical printer.

Scenario:

Burke Properties uses labels to address company mailings. To mail your letters, you'll need address labels to go along with them.

What You Do	How You Do It
1. **Create a new Avery 2160 label document as the main merge document.**	a. **Click the New Blank Document button** to open a new blank document.
	b. **Choose Tools→Letters And Mailings→ Mail Merge** to open the Mail Merge task pane.
	c. **Select Labels.**
	d. **Click Next: Starting Document** to advance to the Step 2 Mail Merge task pane.
	e. **Verify that Change Document Layout is selected and click Label Options.**
	f. The default label is an Avery 2160. **Click OK** to convert the document to a sheet of labels.
2. **Select Mailing List as the data source.**	a. **Click Next: Select Recipients** to move to the Step 3 Mail Merge task pane.
	b. **Verify that Use An Existing List is selected and click Browse.**
	c. **Select the My Documents folder and open Mailing List.xls.**
	d. In the Select Table dialog box, **click OK** to open Sheet 1 of the Excel workbook as the data source.

3. Sort the data source by recipients' last name, and filter the data source to include only customers in New York State.

   a. In the Mail Merge Recipients dialog box, click the **LastName column heading** to sort the list alphabetically by last name.

    Click the words in the heading, not the drop-down arrow.

   b. **Click the drop-down arrow next to the State column heading.**

   c. **Select (Advanced).**

   d. In the Filter and Sort dialog box, on the Filter Records tab, **click the Field drop-down arrow.**

   e. **Select State.**

   f. In the Compare To text box, **enter *NY***

   g. **Click OK.**

   h. In the Mail Merge Recipients dialog box, click **OK.**

---

4. Insert the address block with no title and no company name in all the labels.

   a. **Click Next: Arrange Your Labels** to move to the Step 4 Mail Merge task pane.

   b. **Verify that the insertion point is on the empty paragraph mark in the first label on the page.**

   c. Under Arrange Your Labels, **click Address Block** to open the Insert Address Block dialog box.

   d. From the Insert Recipient's Name In This Format list, **select the choice for first and last name with no title.**

   e. **Uncheck Insert Company Name.**

f. **Click OK** to insert the address block field in the first label.

«AddressBlock»¶

«Next·Record»¶

«Next·Record»¶

«Next·Record»¶

g. **Point to the down arrow at the bottom of the task pane** to scroll down.

h. Under Replicate Labels, **click Update All Labels** to copy the AddressBlock field to the other labels on the page.

«AddressBlock»¶

«Next·Record»«AddressBlock»¶

«Next·Record»«AddressBlock»¶

«Next·Record»«AddressBlock»¶

---

5. **Exclude Elizabeth Milko as a recipient.**

a. **Click Next: Preview Your Labels** to move to the Step 5 Mail Merge task pane.

b. There is no Exclude This Recipient button for labels. **Click Edit Recipient List** to display the Mail Merge Recipients dialog box.

c. **Uncheck the check box for Elizabeth Milko.**

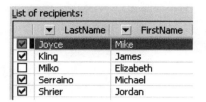

d. **Click OK.**

6. **Print the labels.**

a. **Click Next: Complete The Merge to move to the Step 6 Mail Merge task pane.**

b. **Click Print.**

c. **Verify that All is selected and click OK to open the Print dialog box.**

d. **Click OK to send the labels to the default printer.**

e. **Close the Mail Merge task pane.**

f. **Close the document without saving changes.**

Procedure Reference: Merge Envelopes

To merge envelopes:

1. Open a blank document.

2. Open the Mail Merge task pane, select Envelopes, and click Next: Starting Document.

3. Select your envelope document:

   - Verify that Change Document Layout is selected, and click Envelope Options to specify a size for the envelope. The default is Size 10 (4 ⅛" by 9 ½"). Click OK. The document is now formatted as an envelope.

   - Select Start From Existing Document and open the document if you have an envelope document already created.

4. Click Next: Select Recipients.

5. Select the recipients as you would in any mail merge.

6. Click Next: Arrange Your Envelope.

7. Insert the merge fields.

8. Preview, save, or print your merged envelopes as you would in any mail merge.

Printing a Single Envelope

If you want to print a single envelope, choose Tools→Letters And Mailings→ Envelopes And Labels and select the Envelopes tab. Click Add To Document to create a new document section formatted as an envelope. You can then enter the address manually.

OPTIONAL ACTIVITY 10-4

Merging Envelopes

Data Files:

• Mailing List.xls

Setup:

You have a print driver installed and configured as your default printer. You might or might not have a physical printer.

Scenario:

Burke Properties prints addresses directly on envelopes. To mail your letters, you'll need envelopes to go along with them.

What You Do	How You Do It
1. **Create a new number 10 business envelope document as the main merge document.**	a. **Click the New Blank Document button** to open a new blank document.
	b. **Choose Tools→Letters And Mailings→ Mail Merge** to open the Mail Merge task pane.
	c. **Select Envelopes and click Next: Starting Document** to advance to the Step 2 Mail Merge task pane.
	d. **Verify that Change Document Layout is selected and click Envelope Options.**
	e. The default envelope size is a standard number 10 business envelope. **Click OK** to convert the document to an envelope format.

2. **Select Mailing List as the data source.**

   a. **Click Next: Select Recipients** to move to the Step 3 Mail Merge task pane.

   b. **Verify that Use An Existing List is selected and click Browse.**

   c. **Select the My Documents folder and open Mailing List.xls.**

   d. In the Select Table dialog box, **click OK** to open Sheet 1 of the Excel workbook as the data source.

3. **Sort the data source by recipients' last name, and filter the data source to include only customers in New York State.**

   a. In the Mail Merge Recipients dialog box, **click the LastName column heading** to sort the list alphabetically by last name.

   ⚠ Click the words in the heading, not the drop-down arrow.

   b. **Click the drop-down arrow next to the State column heading.**

   c. **Select (Advanced).**

   d. In the Filter And Sort dialog box, on the Filter Records tab, **click the Field drop-down arrow.**

   e. **Select State.**

   f. In the Compare To text box, **enter *NY***

   g. **Click OK.**

   h. In the Mail Merge Recipients dialog box, **click OK.**

4. **Insert the address block with no title and no company name.**

   a. **Click Next: Arrange Your Envelope** to move to the Step 4 Mail Merge task pane.

   b. **Place the insertion point on the empty paragraph mark in the middle of the envelope.**

   c. Under Arrange Your Envelope, **click Address Block** to open the Insert Address Block dialog box.

   d. From the Insert Recipient's Name In This Format list, **select the choice for first and last name with no title.**

   e. **Uncheck Insert Company Name.**

   f. **Click OK** to insert the address block field in the envelope.

5. **Exclude Elizabeth Milko as a recipient.**

   a. **Click Next: Preview Your Envelopes** to move to the Step 5 Mail Merge task pane.

   b. **Click the Next Recipient button twice** to move to the envelope for Elizabeth Milko.

   c. **Click Exclude This Recipient.**

6. **Print the envelopes.**

   a. **Click Next: Complete The Merge** to move to the Step 6 Mail Merge task pane.

   b. **Click Print.**

   c. **Verify that All is selected and click OK** to open the Print dialog box.

   d. **Click OK** to send the envelopes to the default printer.

   e. **Close the Mail Merge task pane.**

   f. **Close the document without saving changes.**

TOPIC D

Use Word to Create a Data Source

In the previous topics, you completed a merge using an existing data source. You can also create your own data sources. In this topic, you'll use Word to create a data source document.

In many cases, your merge data source will already be provided. Maybe you're using your Outlook contacts list; maybe your company has an Access database. However, if none of those data sources already exists, you can use Word to create a personalized data source for yourself. If you know how to structure a data source document in Word, you'll always have the information you need to complete your merges successfully.

How to Use Word to Create a Data Source

Procedure Reference: Create a Data Source in Word

To create a data source in Word:

1. Create a new blank document.

2. Insert a table with the number of columns that equals the number of fields you need for your data source.

3. Enter column headings in each column of the table to create field names. Follow the Data Source Field Name Guidelines.

4. Enter the data in separate rows in the table.

5. Save the document.

6. Test the data source by performing a merge.

Data Source Field Name Guidelines

Use the following guidelines when you create the field names in your data source:

- Make each field name unique within the data source.
- Begin all field names with a letter.
- Make field names as short as possible. Field names cannot exceed 40 characters.
- Do not use spaces in field names.

Creating a Main Merge Document

The only way in which a main merge document differs from an ordinary Word document is that the merge document contains merge fields. Because you can insert merge fields during the merge process, there are no special steps you need to take before the merge to create a main merge document. However, if you prefer, you can insert the fields into the document manually, prior to the merge, by using the Insert→Fields menu choice. See the Microsoft Office Word Help system for more information on inserting merge fields manually.

ACTIVITY 10-5

Creating a Data Source

Scenario:

Jan Burke wants to let three outstanding Burke Properties sales people know that their personal share of their home sales commissions is going to increase. Jan has asked you to prepare the basic documents; Jan will personalize the memos and send them herself.

What You Do	How You Do It
1. Create a new document and enter the fields for the data source.	a. Create a new blank document.
	b. Insert a table with four columns and four rows.
	c. In the first cell in the first column, **enter FName**
	d. In the first cell in the second column, **enter LName**
	e. In the first cell in the third column, **enter Current**
	f. In the first cell in the fourth column, **enter New**

FName¤	LName¤	Current¤	New¤	¤
¤	¤	¤	¤	¤
¤	¤	¤	¤	¤
¤	¤	¤	¤	¤

What You Do	How You Do It
2. Enter the data for Jennifer Allen, whose percentage is increasing from 50% to 55%.	a. In the first cell in the empty second row of the table, **type Jennifer**
	b. In the second cell in the second row of the table, **type Allen**
	c. In the third cell in the second row of the table, **type 50%**
	d. In the fourth cell in the second row of the table, **type 55%**

3. **Enter the data for James Hickey, whose percentage is increasing from 55% to 60%.**

   a. In the first cell in the empty third row of the table, type *James*

   b. In the second cell in the third row of the table, type *Hickey*

   c. In the third cell in the third row of the table, type *55%*

   d. In the fourth cell in the third row of the table, type *60%*

4. **Enter the data for Michelle Robinson, whose percentage is increasing from 50% to 60%.**

   a. In the first cell in the last row of the table, type *Michelle*

   b. In the second cell in the last row of the table, type *Robinson*

   c. In the third cell in the last row of the table, type *50%*

   d. In the fourth cell in the last row of the table, type *60%*

5. **Save the data source as *My Data Source* and close the document.**

   a. Save the document as *My Data Source*

   b. Close the document.

ACTIVITY 10-6

Testing the Data Source

Data Files:

- Commission Memo.doc

Scenario:

You've created the memo and the data source for Jan. Jan just wants to personalize the final product. You want to be sure the documents can merge successfully, because then Jan can simply resume the merge at a later time to personalize the memos as she wishes.

What You Do	How You Do It
1. Select Commission Memo as the main merge document.	a. Open Commission Memo.
	b. This memo needs the agent's names added to the To line, and the old and new commission rates on their own lines in the body of the memo. **Choose Tools→ Letters And Mailings→Mail Merge.**
	c. **Verify that Letters is selected and click Next: Starting Document.**
	d. **Verify that Use The Current Document is selected and click Next: Select Recipients.**
2. Select the data source.	a. **Verify that Use An Existing List is selected and click Browse.**
	b. **Select the My Documents folder.**
	c. **Open My Data Source** to display your data source data in the Mail Merge Recipients dialog box.

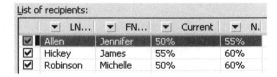

	How You Do It (cont.)
	d. **Click OK** to close the Mail Merge Recipients dialog box.

3. **Insert a greeting line on the To line.**

   a. **Click Next: Write Your Letter.**

   b. **Place the insertion point on the blank paragraph mark on the To line in the memo.**

   c. **Click Greeting Line** to open the Greeting Line dialog box.

   d. In the Greeting Line Format area, from the first drop-down list, **select (none).**

      The word To is already in the memo, so you do not need to include a salutation in the field.

   e. From the second drop-down list, **select the format with first and last names and no title.**

   f. From the last drop-down list, **select (none).**

Greeting line format:
| (none) | Joshua Randall Jr. | (none) |

    You do not need punctuation to follow the To line in a memo.

   g. **Click OK** to close the Greeting Line dialog box and insert the greeting line field in the memo.

   To: → «GreetingLine»¶

4. **Insert a field for the current commission rate.**

   a. **Place the insertion point on the first blank paragraph mark in the body of the memo.**

   b. This is the line for the current commission rate. **Click More Items** to open the Insert Merge Field dialog box.

c. In the Insert area, Database Fields is selected. **Select Current and click Insert.**

d. **Click Close** to close the Insert Merge Field dialog box and view the field in the memo.

«Current»¶

to:¶

---

5. **Insert a field for the new commission rate.**

a. **Place the insertion point on the remaining blank paragraph mark in the body of the memo.**

b. This is the line for the new commission rate. **Click More Items.**

c. **Select New and click Insert.**

d. **Click Close.**

«Current»¶

to:¶

«New»¶

---

6. **Preview the documents.**

a. **Click Next: Preview Your Letters** to view Jennifer Allen's current and new commission rates in the body of the memo.

b. **Press Page Up** to scroll to the top of the current document and view Jennifer Allen's name on the To line.

c. **Click the Next Recipient arrow twice** to preview the other documents.

---

7. **Save the main merge document as** *My Commission Memo*

     Saving the merge document enables you to resume the merge and complete and print the memos at a later time.

a. **Choose File→Save As.**

b. **Save the document as** *My Commission Memo*

c. **Close the Mail Merge task pane.**

d. **Close My Commission Memo.**

Lesson 10 Follow-up

In this lesson, you performed mail merges to produce a variety of merge documents. Once you know how to perform all the steps of a merge successfully, you will probably find many applications for the mail merge technique. Think of using a merge any time you have documents that share most of the same text; chances are, you'll be able to set up a merge and produce all the customized documents you need in a fraction of the time it would take to type each one individually.

1. **Name some examples of mail merge output you've seen in your personal experience.**

2. **How do you think you will use mail merge in your work situation?**

Follow-up

In this course, you created customized efficiency tools in Microsoft® Word 2003, and increased the complexity of your Microsoft® Word 2003 documents by adding customized lists, tables, charts, and graphics. The skills you gained in this course will help you as you prepare for the Microsoft Office Specialist exams for Microsoft® Word 2003. These skills will also help you in your day-to-day work with Microsoft® Word 2003, as you create more attractive and effective documents with less effort than before.

What's Next?

Microsoft Word 2003: Level 3 is the next course in this series. In that course, you will learn a variety of techniques for working with and collaborating on large documents and for using Microsoft® Word 2003 to design and develop content for the World Wide Web.

NOTES

APPENDIX A

Microsoft Office Specialist Program

Selected Element K courseware addresses Microsoft Office Specialist skills. The following tables indicate where Word 2003 skills are covered. For example, 1-3 indicates the lesson and activity number applicable to that skill.

Core Skill Sets and Skills Being Measured	Word 2003: Level 1	Word 2003: Level 2	Word 2003: Level 3
Insert and edit text, symbols and special characters			
Inserting text, symbols, hidden text and special characters	1-4, 2-3, 7-1, 1-Lab, 2-Lab, 5-Lab	8-2	5-3
Deleting, cutting, copying, pasting text and using the clipboard	2-6, 2-7, 2-8, 2-Lab		
Checking spelling and grammar	5-3, 4-Lab		
Checking language usage (e.g., Thesaurus)	5-1, 5-Lab		
Insert Frequently Used and Pre-defined Text			
Creating text for repeated use (e.g., AutoText)	2-5		
Inserting pre-defined text (e.g., AutoText and AutoCorrect)	1-4, 2-5		
Inserting date and time fields	8-5		
Navigate to Specific Content			
Finding and replacing text	2-10	2-Lab	
Moving to selected content (e.g., Select Browse Object, Go To)			2-8, 3-3
Insert, Position, and Size Graphics			
Inserting, positioning, and sizing graphics, text boxes, and shapes	7-2, 6-Lab	6-1, 6-2, 6-3, 7-3, 5-Lab, 6-Lab	
Create and Modify Diagrams and Charts			

Core Skill Sets and Skills Being Measured	Word 2003: Level 1	Word 2003: Level 2	Word 2003: Level 3
Creating and modifying charts and diagrams		2-7, 2-8, 6-4, 2-Lab	
Locate, Select, and Insert Supporting Information			
Locating supporting information in local reference materials or on the Internet using the Research too.	5-1		1-6
Using the Research tool to select and insert supporting text-based information	5-1		1-6
Insert and Modify Tables			
Inserting new tables	6-1, 6-Lab		
Converting text to tables	6-6, 6-Lab		
Applying pre-defined formats to tables (e.g., Autoformats)	6-5, 6-Lab		
Modifying table borders and shading	6-5	2-5	
Revising tables (insert and delete rows and columns, modify cell formats)		2-2, 2-Lab	
Create Bulleted Lists, Numbered Lists, and Outlines			
Customizing and applying bullets and numbering	4-6	1-4, 1-5	
Creating outlines		1-4	
Insert and Modify Hyperlinks			
Inserting and modifying hyperlinks to other documents and Web pages			6-2
Format Text			
Finding and modifying font typeface, style, color and size	3-7, 3-Lab	4-1, 4-Lab	
Applying styles to and clearing styles from text, tables, and lists	3-6, 4-5, 4-Lab	4-1, 4-3, 4-4, 4-Lab	
Applying highlights to text	3-4, 3-Lab		
Applying text effects		3-2, 3-Lab	
Modifying character spacing		3-1	
Format Paragraphs			
Applying borders and shading to paragraphs	4-4, 4-Lab		
Indenting, spacing, and aligning paragraphs	4-2, 4-3, 4-7, 4-Lab	2-Lab	
Setting, removing, and modifying tab stops	4-1, 4-Lab		
Apply and Format Columns			
Applying and formatting columns		7-2, 7-Lab	

Core Skill Sets and Skills Being Measured	Word 2003: Level 1	Word 2003: Level 2	Word 2003: Level 3
Insert and Modify Content in Headers and Footers			
Inserting and modifying content in document headers and footers	8-5, 8-Lab	8-2	
Inserting and formatting page numbers	8-5, 8-6		
Modify Document Layout and Page Setup			
Inserting and deleting breaks	2-3, 8-7, 8-8	7-1, 7-2, 7-Lab	
Modifying page margins and page orientation	8-1, 8-2, 8-Lab		
Circulate Documents for Review			
Sending documents for review via e-mail			2-4
Sending documents in an e-mail or as an e-mail attachment			1-7, 1-Lab
Compare and Merge Documents			
Comparing and merging documents			2-6, 2-7, 2-Lab
Insert, View, and Edit Comments			
Inserting, viewing, and editing comments			2-5, 2-8, 2-Lab
Track, Accept, and Reject Proposed Changes			
Locating successive changes in a document			2-8, 2-Lab
Tracking, accepting, and rejecting changes			2-5, 2-8, 2-Lab
Create New Documents Using Templates			
Creating new document types using templates		9-1, 9-3, 9-Lab	
Review and Modify Document Properties			
Reviewing and modifying the document summary			2-1, 5-1, 5-2
Reviewing word, paragraph, and character counts (e.g., Word Count)	5-5, 5-Lab		
Organize Documents Using File Folders			
Creating and using folders for document storage	1-5		
Renaming folders	8-1		
Saving Documents in Appropriate Formats for Different Uses			
Converting documents to different formats for transportability (e.g., .rtf, .txt)			1-5, 6-1, 1-Lab
Saving documents as Web pages			6-1
Print Documents, Envelopes, and Labels			

APPENDIX A

Core Skill Sets and Skills Being Measured	Word 2003: Level 1	Word 2003: Level 2	Word 2003: Level 3
Printing documents, envelopes, and labels	1-7	10-3, 10-4	
Preview Documents and Web Pages			
Previewing a document for printing	1-6, 5-6, 1-Lab, 5-Lab	2-Lab	
Previewing a Web page for publication			6-1
Change and Organize Documents Views and Windows			
Revealing formatting and hidden text	3-6		5-3, 5-Lab
Viewing reading layout, normal, outline, full screen, and zoom views	1-6, 5-6, 8-8, 5-Lab		1-3, 2-8
Showing/hiding white space in a document	8-7		
Splitting windows and arrange panes			2-3, 4-6

Expert Skill Sets and Skills Being Measured	Word 2003: Level 1	Word 2003: Level 2	Word 2003: Level 3
Create Custom Styles for Text, Tables, and Lists			
Creating and applying custom styles for text, tables, and lists		4-1, 4-2, 4-3, 4-4, 4-Lab	
Control Pagination			
Controlling orphans and widows		3-3	
Setting line and page breaks	2-3, 8-7, 8-8		
Format, Position, and Resize Graphics Using Advanced Layout Features			
Wrapping text with graphics		5-3, 6-1, 6-3	
Cropping and rotating graphics		5-2	
Controlling image contrast and brightness		5-1	
Scaling and resizing graphics	7-2	5-2	
Insert and Modify Objects			
Inserting and modifying new objects and objects from files			1-1, 1-2, 1-Lab
Create and Modify Diagrams and Charts Using Data From Other Sources			
Creating and revising charts using data from other sources (e.g., Excel)			1-2
Sort Content in Lists and Tables			
Sorting content in lists and tables by specific categories		1-1, 1-2, 2-1, 1-Lab, 2-Lab	

Expert Skill Sets and Skills Being Measured	Word 2003: Level 1	Word 2003: Level 2	Word 2003: Level 3
Perform calculations in tables			
Using formulas in tables		2-6, 2-Lab	
Modify Table Formats			
Modifying table formats by merging and/or splitting table cells		2-3	
Modifying text position and direction in a cell		2-4, 2-Lab	
Modifying table properties		2-4, 4-4	
Inserting and modifying fields		9-7	
Summarize Document Content Using Automated Tools			
Summarize relevant content using automated tools (e.g., AutoSummarize)			4-8
Analyzing content readability using automated tools (e.g., Readability Statistics)	5-2		
Use Automated Tools for Document Navigation			
Inserting Bookmarks			3-1, 3-Lab
Using automation features for document navigation (e.g., Document Map, Thumbnails)			2-8, 3-2, 3-4, 4-2, 4-4
Merge Letters With Other Data Sources			
Completing an entire mail merge process for form letters		10-6, 10-Lab	
Merge Labels With Other Data Sources			
Completing an entire mail merge process for mailing labels		10-2, 10-3, 10-5, 10-6	
Structure Documents Using XML			
Adding, deleting, updating, and modifying schemas, solutions, and settings in the Schema Library			8-1, 8-5, 8-Lab
Adding, deleting, and modifying schemas and transforms to documents			8-1, 8-4, 8-5, 8-Lab
Managing elements and attributes in XML documents (e.g., adding, changing, deleting, cutting, copying)			8-2
Defining XML options (e.g., applying schema validation options, applying XML view options)			8-2, 8-3, 8-Lab
Create and Modify Forms			
Creating and modifying forms			7-1

Expert Skill Sets and Skills Being Measured	Word 2003: Level 1	Word 2003: Level 2	Word 2003: Level 3
Setting and changing options on form fields and check boxes			7-1
Create and Modify Document Background			
Creating watermarks	7-3, 7-Lab		
Applying themes			6-4
Creating and modifying document background colors and fill effects			6-4
Create and Modify Document Indexes and Tables			
Creating and modifying document indexes, tables of content, figures, and authorities			4-2, 4-3, 4-5, 4-6, 4-Lab
Insert and Modify Endnotes, Footnotes, Captions, and Crossreferences			
Inserting format and modifying endnotes, footnotes, captions, and crossreferences			3-2, 3-3, 3-4, 3-Lab
Formatting numbering and marks for footnotes and endnotes			3-2
Create and Manage Master Documents and Subdocuments			
Creating master documents with three or more subdocuments			4-7, 4-Lab
Modify Track Changes Options			
Setting reviewer's ink colors, setting balloon options, showing and hiding reviewers			2-5, 2-8
Publish and Edit Web Documents			
Setting Web options and saving to a Web server			6-1
Inserting and modifying frames			6-5
Manage Document Versions			
Creating, viewing, deleting versions of documents			2-2, 2-Lab
Protect and Restrict Forms and Documents			
Setting formatting restrictions			5-4
Setting editing restrictions			5-5, 7-2, 5-Lab
Adding users excepted from restrictions (groups and individuals)			5-5
Applying passwords to documents and forms			5-7, 7-2, 5-Lab
Attach Digital Signatures to Documents			
Using digital signatures to authenticate documents			5-6
Customize Document Properties			

Expert Skill Sets and Skills Being Measured	Word 2003: Level 1	Word 2003: Level 2	Word 2003: Level 3
Inserting and editing summary and custom information in document properties			2-1, 5-1, 5-2, 5-Lab
Create, Edit, and Run Macros			
Creating and running macros		8-1, 8-2, 8-Lab	
Editing a macro using the Visual Basic Editor		8-3, 8-Lab	
Customize Menus and Toolbars			
Creating a custom menu		8-6	
Adding and removing buttons from a toolbar		8-4, 8-5, 8-Lab	
Modify Word Default Settings			
Changing the default file location for templates		9-5	
Setting default dictionary	5-4		
Modifying default font settings		9-4	

NOTES

LESSON LABS

Due to classroom setup constraints, some labs cannot be keyed in sequence immediately following their associated lesson. Your instructor will tell you whether your labs can be practiced immediately following the lesson or whether they require separate setup from the main lesson content.

LESSON 1 LAB 1

Managing Lists

Activity Time:

10 minutes

Data Files:

- BB Sales Lists.doc

Scenario:

You're a marketing assistant for Books And Beyond, a retail chain that combines a book and music store with an in-store coffee shop. You're preparing a document for the monthly sales associates' meeting. There are two lists in the document: one shows CD sales by category, and one shows the top 10 customer book favorites. In the first list, you want to show how CD sales for the country music category relate to CD sales for the other music categories, and you realize that this relationship is hard to see with the list in its current order. You have almost completed the second list, when you realize that the list would look better if the numbers lined up directly under the column heading, *Title*. You also want to add some commentary text after the ninth book entry, noting that this book appeared on the readers' poll for the first time this month. Then you can complete the list with the number-10 title, "Dillon," by Jennifer Singles.

 You can find a sample solution to this activity in the Final BB Sales Lists document in the Solutions folder in the student data file location.

1. In the BB Sales Lists document, **sort the music-categories list in descending order by CD Sales.**

2. Modify the placement of the numbers in the Top 10 Book Favorites list so that the numbers align with the column heading *Title* above them.

3. Add a comment paragraph in your own words to follow the ninth entry in the Top 10 Book Favorites list.

4. Add the title and author for the tenth entry on the list.

5. Save the completed document as *My BB Sales Lists* and close the document.

Lesson 2 Lab 1

Customizing a Table and Chart

Activity Time:

20 minutes

Data Files:

*   BB Music Table.doc

Scenario:

You're preparing a document for the monthly Books And Beyond sales associates' meeting, with a table that shows CD and tape sales for various music categories. You've put in the raw sales data, and now you need to complete the table with a column showing sales totals for each category. You want to show the sales people which are the top categories according to total sales.

After you complete the data entry, you want to make some changes to the appearance of the table. For one thing, there seems to be too much white space in the table columns. Also, you think that numeric data looks better when it lines up to the left, rather than to the right like text. Because of the recent country-music promotion, you want to emphasize the country-music category in the table. And there's nothing to show the overall purpose of the table, which is to show the top music categories; it could use a title with that information.

Your last step is to make it easier to see the relationships between CD and tape sales in each category in a graphical way. You want to show how each music category contributes to the overall sales for CDs and for tapes.

 You can find a sample solution to this activity in the Final BB Music Table document in the Solutions folder in the student data file location.

1. In the BB Music Table document, **insert a TOTAL SALES column at the right of the table.**

2. Create formulas to show the total sales amounts for each category.

3. Sort the table in descending order by total sales.

4. Adjust the column widths to fit the table data.

5. Right-align the numbers in the last three columns of the table.

6. Add shading of your choice to the Country row.

7. Create a new title row for the table containing the text *TOP MUSIC CATEGO-RIES* centered across the other columns in the table.

8. Create a chart from the Category, CD Sales, and Tape Sales data.

9. Select a stacked-column chart type.

10. Add a chart title that reads *CD and Tape Sales Comparison*.

11. Move and size the chart appropriately.

12. Preview the document.

13. Save the completed document as *My BB Music Table* and close the document.

LESSON 3 LAB 1

Customizing Formatting

Activity Time:

10 minutes

Data Files:

- BB Format.doc

Scenario:

You're preparing a marketing flyer to promote Books And Beyond's merchandise and services. You've laid out the text and formatting for the flyer, but you feel there are a couple of areas where it needs something special. For one thing, you want to add a special touch to the appearance of the overall flyer title; it looks too similar to the main titles in the document. You want it to have a different, customized look, not merely to make it bigger. And, you'd like to add a whimsical touch to the word "Beyond" in the document title. You also know that some of your customers will see an electronic version of this flyer, so you can add some animation to the top section to help catch their eyes.

When you proofread the document, you realize that the section on Easy Listening starts on one page and finishes on the second page. It would be better if this section always stayed at the start of a new page.

 You can find a sample solution to this activity in the Final BB Format document in the Solutions folder in the student data file location.

1. In the BB Format document, **configure the text of the main title of the document to scale to 150%.**

2. **Raise the word "Beyond" in the document title by 5 pt.**

3. **Add an animated text effect of your choice to the document title and subtitle.**

4. **Configure the "Easy Listening" section title paragraph so that it will always start on a new page.**

5. **Preview the document.**

6. **Save the completed document as** *My BB Format* **and close the document.**

LESSON 4 LAB 1

Creating Custom Styles

Activity Time:

15 minutes

Data Files:

- BB Styles.doc
- BB List.doc

Scenario:

You're preparing a marketing flyer to promote Books And Beyond's merchandise and services. You've laid out the text and formatting for the flyer. You'd like the section headings in the flyer to be similar in style to the main heading, but not quite as large. If you can create a look you like, you'll want to have a way to apply it easily to all the section headings in this document, and possibly in other new documents.

Your boss has also asked you to send her a short document with a list of Books And Beyond's special services, which include free delivery, "Meet the Author" Events, and rare book searches (both locally and using the Internet). You want this list to look great and catch the customer's eye. You have an existing document with a good-looking list in it, and you would like to be able to save that list format and apply it to your new list document.

You can find a sample solution to this activity in the Final BB Styles and the Final BB List documents in the Solutions folder in the student data file location.

1. In the BB Styles document, **format the What Is Books And Beyond? title to be centered, small caps, and not italic.**

2. **Create a BB Heading paragraph style from the formatted text and add the style to the Normal template.**

3. **Apply the BB Heading style to the other two section titles in the document.**

4. **Save the completed document as *My BB Styles* and close the document.**

5. **Create a new BB List style based on the list in the BB List document, and add the style to the Normal template.**

6. **Save the document as *My BB List Style* and close the document.**

7. **Open a new, blank document.**

8. **Enter a heading that reads *Our Special Services* and press Enter to create a blank paragraph.**

9. **Format the Our Special Services heading text with the BB Heading style.**

10. **Apply the BB List style to the blank paragraph and enter the three main items for the bullet list.**

11. **Add sub-items for the two types of rare book searches.**

12. **Save the completed document as *My BB List* and close the document.**

LESSON 5 LAB 1

Modifying a Picture

Activity Time:

10 minutes

Data Files:

- BB Picture.doc

Scenario:

You're working with a promotional document for Books And Beyond. You found a great piece of Clip Art on the Microsoft Office Web site and inserted it into your document. However, its current placement disrupts the flow of the text too much—it would be better to set the picture off to the side and let the text wrap around it. After you do, you decide that the text looks a bit too ragged; you can smooth out the look by adding some white space to the picture. Finally, you would like the picture to look lighter and more cheerful, so you think you might need to brighten it up a bit.

 You can find a sample solution to this activity in the Final BB Picture document in the Solutions folder in the student data file location.

1. In the BB Picture document, **set the layout properties for the picture to Square, and set the horizontal alignment to Right.**

2. **Crop the picture to add white space to the left side and bottom.**

3. **Change the Brightness setting for the picture to 60%.**

4. **Save the completed document as *My BB Picture* and close the document.**

LESSON 6 LAB 1

Customizing Graphics

Activity Time:

15 minutes

Data Files:

- BB Graphics.doc

Scenario:

You're working with a promotional document for Books And Beyond. You have the text entered in the document and now you want to create some visual interest. You can see at least three places where some graphic elements could enhance the document. One is to create a more decorative overall title for the document. The next is to highlight the subtitle, "What Is Books & Beyond?" by adding a graphic background. The other is to create a diagram that displays the main idea of the text—that the Books & Beyond experience builds on its foundation as a respected bookseller by adding best-selling music and a popular coffee bar.

 You can find a sample solution to this activity in the Final BB Graphics document in the Solutions folder in the student data file location.

1. In the BB Graphics document, **replace the Books & Beyond title with a piece of WordArt that reads** *Books & Beyond*. Select any WordArt style and formatting properties you choose.

2. **Draw an AutoShape of your choice with a fill color of your choice around the "What Is Books & Beyond?" text.**

3. **Set the layout properties for the AutoShape to Behind Text.**

4. **Insert a pyramid diagram at the beginning of the "Some people say...." paragraph.**

5. **Insert the text elements for the three components of the pyramid diagram:** *Coffee Bar*, *Music*, and *Books*.

6. **Set the size of the diagram to approximately three inches square.**

7. **Set the Layout properties for the diagram to Square, Right.**

8. **Format the text in each section of the diagram so that the font size increases with the size of each diagram section.**

9. **Preview the document.**

10. **Save the completed document as *My BB Graphics* and close the document.**

LESSON 7 LAB 1

Controlling Text Flow

Activity Time:

15 minutes

Data Files:

- BB Newsletter.doc

Scenario:

Your supervisor has handed you text for the first issue of the new Books & Beyond newsletter and has asked you to format the text flow in the newsletter appropriately. Most newsletters you've seen use a two column format, and you think this will work for this information. However, there are two areas of the document that will not work well in columns because they are too wide: the masthead section at the beginning of the document, and the tables at the end of the document that list current bestsellers.

 You can find a sample solution to this activity in the Final BB Newsletter document in the Solutions folder in the student data file location.

1. **In the BB Newsletter document, insert a continuous section break at the beginning of the "Have you ever..." paragraph.**

2. **Insert a Next Page section break at the beginning of the Bestsellers Lists heading at the bottom of the first page.**

3. **Format Section 2 into two equal columns with a line between.**

4. **Insert a column break before the "Best Sellers and the Classics" heading at the bottom of the first column.**

5. **Preview the document.**

6. **Save the completed document as *My BB Newsletter* and close the document.**

LESSON 8 LAB 1

Automating a Task

Activity Time:

20 minutes

Data Files:

- BB Macro.doc
- BB Macro Test.doc
- BB Edit Test.doc

Scenario:

Books & Beyond has recently revised its corporate communications standards. Previously, it was acceptable to refer to the company as either "Books And Beyond," or "Books & Beyond." Now, the company wants the name to appear consistently as "Books & Beyond." The company has asked you to include the company name at the bottom of every document you create as well. You would like to find a quick and easy way to comply with these requirements.

 You can find a sample solution to this activity in the Final BB Macro document in the Solutions folder in the student data file location.

---

1. In the BB Macro document, **create a new macro named BB_Name, stored in the Normal template.**

2. **Record the macro as you replace all instances of "Books And Beyond" with the text *Books & Beyond*. Continue recording as you create a footer containing the left-aligned text *Books & Beyond*.**

3. **Stop recording the macro.**

4. **Save the document as *My BB Macro* and close the document.**

5. In the BB Macro Test document, **run the BB Name macro to test it.**

6. **Save the document as *My BB Macro Test*.**

7. **Preview the document.**

8. You decide that the footer looks unbalanced. **Edit the macro to insert a vbTab character in the footer to center the footer text.**

9. In the document, **delete the existing footer.**

10. **Run the modified macro to test your modification.**

11. **Preview the document.**

12. **Add the macro to a toolbar button on the Standard toolbar, using your own choice of image and button text.**

13. **Save and close the document.**

14. In the BB Edit Test document, **run the edited macro from the toolbar button to test it.**

15. **Save the document as** *My BB Edit Test* **and close the document.**

LESSON 9 LAB 1

Creating Documents Automatically

Activity Time:

20 minutes

Scenario:

As the Books & Beyond store manager, you run a brief staff meeting once a week at 9:00 A.M., before the store opens. You always include 10-minute presentations on sales promotions, sales results, and the employee of the week. Because the meetings are brief and simple, you don't take minutes or keep a formal record of attendees. Tomorrow morning, the meeting will be held in the Sound Lounge, but sometimes the meeting is held in other locations.

You would like to have a nice-looking agenda to hand out at tomorrow's meeting without having to do a lot of work designing the document. After you create the agenda document, you realize that you can reuse most of the agenda information from week to week, because the only things that change are the date, location, and occasionally an additional agenda item or two. You would like to have an easy way to re-create the agenda for yourself without re-entering the repeated information.

 You can find a sample solution to this activity in the Final BB Agenda document and the Final BB Agenda Template template in the Solutions folder in the student data file location.

1. **Use the Agenda Wizard to create an agenda in a style of your choice. Include the meeting title, time, date, location, and three agenda items.** You can include other information in the agenda if you wish.

2. **Save the agenda document as** *My BB Agenda*.

3. In My BB Agenda, **replace the meeting date and meeting location with MacroButton fields that prompt the user for date and location information.**

4. The list of agenda topics is a table with no gridlines. **Insert a new row at the bottom of the Agenda Topics table and insert MacroButton fields in each cell in the new row to prompt for agenda item, presenter name, and time.** (The order of the cells in the table will vary depending upon the agenda style you selected.)

5. **Save the document in the default template location as a document template named** *My BB Agenda Template*, **and close all open documents.**

6. **Test My BB Agenda Template by creating a new agenda document based on the new template.**

7. **Save the new document as** *My BB Agenda Test* **and close the document.**

LESSON 10 LAB 1

Merging Letters and Envelopes

Activity Time:

20 minutes

Data Files:

- BB Form Letter.doc

Scenario:

The Books & Beyond store manager has asked you to send out a form letter welcoming three new customers who have just joined the Books & Beyond Reading Rewards sales incentive program. The form letter is on the store computer, but the manager has given you the new customer's names written down on a piece of paper. You need to create and print letters with each customer's name and address, and to print envelopes to go along with the letters. The manager has asked you to provide her with a hard copy of the letters to sign, and an electronic copy for her files.

 You can find a sample solution to this activity in the Final BB Data Source and the Final BB Merge Output documents in the Solutions folder in the student data file location.

1. In a new, blank Word document, **create a table to use as a data source containing three first names, last names, street addresses, city names, states, and ZIP codes of your choice.**

2. **Save the data source document as** *My BB Data Source* **and close the document.**

3. In a blank document, **use the Mail Merge task pane to select BB Form Letter as the main document, My BB Data Source as the data source, and to insert the address block and greeting line fields.** For best layout, put the address block on the first blank paragraph mark after the date, and put the greeting line on the blank paragraph mark immediately above the body of the letter.

4. **Complete the merge and print the merged output.**

5. **Save the merge output document as** *My BB Merge Output* **and close any open documents.**

6. **Run Mail Merge again to create an envelope document, select My BB Data Source as the data source, and insert an address block field into the envelope.**

7. **Print the merged envelopes.**

8. **Close all open documents without saving changes.**

SOLUTIONS

Lesson 2

Activity 2-2

2. How else could you get the new row into the correct location in the table?

Insert the row anywhere in the table and sort the table.

Activity 2-6

2. Can you use AutoSum for the totals for the remaining rows? Why or why not?

No, you cannot, because now that there is a number in the Principal row, AutoSum will default to a =SUM(ABOVE) and create a column total instead of performing a =SUM(LEFT) to perform a row total.

Lesson 7

Activity 7-1

2. How can you tell what section you are in?

The "SEC" indicator on the status bar displays the number of the section containing the insertion point.

Lesson 8

Activity 8-1

2. How does the company name appear in the document?

Burke Properties, and Burke Properties Inc.

4. How does the company name now appear in the document?

Burke Properties™

Activity 8-2

1. **You need to plan your macro. What are the general steps you must take to create the macro?**

    Create and name the macro; choose View→Header And Footer; switch to the footer; enter the footer information.

2. **Does this macro require that you record mouse movements?**

    No, it does not.

Activity 8-3

4. **How could you update the footer in the current document?**

    You could edit the existing footer manually, or you could delete the footer and run the modified BurkeFooter macro.

Lesson 10

Activity 10-1

2. **What do you need to insert into this document to convert it to a main merge document?**

    You must insert merge fields to link this document to a data source.

3. **After you complete the merge, where should the variable information appear in this letter?**

    After the date and before the body of the letter.

5. **How many fields are there in this data source? What are the fields?**

    Six fields: FirstName, LastName, Address1, City, State, and Zip.

6. **What order do the rows appear in?**

    Alphabetically by first name.

7. **True or False? The data source contains rows of information only for customers in New York State.**

    ___ True

    _✓_ False

9. **What two merge fields were inserted into the main merge document to link it to the data source?**

    AddressBlock and GreetingLine.

10. **Recipients from which states are included in this merged mailing?**

    States in the Northeast.

11. **In what order do the mail merge letters appear?**

Alphabetically by recipient's last name.

NOTES

GLOSSARY

arguments
The numeric values in a table formula.

brightness
The setting on a graphic element that controls the amount of white in the colors or shades of gray in the image.

cell merge
Combining a group of adjacent cells into a single, larger cell.

cell split
Dividing a single cell into a group of adjacent cells.

contrast
The setting on a graphic element that controls the difference between adjacent colors or shades of gray in the image.

data source
The merge component that contains the variable information for the mail merge.

delimited text file
A plain text file in which fields and rows are separated by standard characters.

document templates
Templates used to create specific kinds of documents.

document wizard
A miniature application that uses a multi-page format to guide users through the process of creating standard business documents based on templates.

drawing canvas
Word's workspace for grouping, moving, and resizing drawn objects.

field codes
Programming instructions that tell Word how to determine the results of a field.

floating graphic
A graphic in the drawing layer that can be positioned anywhere.

function
The mathematical operator portion of a table formula.

global templates
Templates whose settings are available to all open Word documents.

inline graphic
A graphic that is positioned with the text at the insertion point.

mail merge
The process of linking static information contained in one document (the main document) with variable information contained in another document (the data source) to produce multiple unique documents with the same basic common structure.

main merge document
The merge component that contains the static text and formatting.

merge fields
Placeholder areas in a main merge document that link the main merge document to the relevant variable information in the data source.

module
A VBA code block containing one or more macros.

Glossary

orphan

A single line of a multiline paragraph that appears by itself at the bottom of a page or column.

outline numbered list

A list with items on multiple levels where the number or bullet format is different for the different levels.

point

A measuring unit of type size; approximately 1/72 of an inch.

section

A portion of a document that can have page layout options set independently from other portions of the document.

section break

The divider between sections of a document.

sort field

An individual item, set off by a field separator character, that you can sort by in a list item or table column.

template

A special type of Word document with a .dot file extension, that is used as a basis for creating other new documents.

text box

A graphic entity that serves as a container for text or for other graphics.

widow

A single line of a multiline paragraph that appears by itself at the top of a page or column.

INDEX